Inside My Soul
Poetry from the Heart

_____

© Copyright 2004 Shirley A. Jackson.
All rights reserved. No part of this publication may be reproduced, stored in a retrieval system, or transmitted, in any form or by any means, electronic, mechanical, photocopying, recording, or otherwise, without the written prior permission of the author.

Note for Librarians: a cataloguing record for this book that includes Dewey Decimal Classification and US Library of Congress numbers is available from the Library and Archives of Canada. The complete cataloguing record can be obtained from their online database at:
www.collectionscanada.ca/amicus/index-e.html
ISBN 1-4120-4207-0

TRAFFORD

Offices in Canada, USA, Ireland, UK and Spain

This book was published on-demand in cooperation with Trafford Publishing. On-demand publishing is a unique process and service of making a book available for retail sale to the public taking advantage of on-demand manufacturing and Internet marketing. On-demand publishing includes promotions, retail sales, manufacturing, order fulfilment, accounting and collecting royalties on behalf of the author.

Book sales for North America and international:
Trafford Publishing, 6E–2333 Government St.,
Victoria, BC V8T 4P4 CANADA
phone 250 383 6864 (toll-free 1 888 232 4444)
fax 250 383 6804; email to orders@trafford.com

Book sales in Europe:
Trafford Publishing (UK) Ltd., Enterprise House, Wistaston Road Business Centre,
Wistaston Road, Crewe, Cheshire CW2 7RP UNITED KINGDOM
phone 01270 251 396 (local rate 0845 230 9601)
facsimile 01270 254 983; orders.uk@trafford.com

Order online at:
www.trafford.com/robots/04-2014.html

10 9 8 7 6 5 4 3 2 1

ACKNOWLEDGEMENTS

First giving honor to God who made all things possible. God has been the beacon in my life and has never failed me. Thank you my Heavenly Father.

To my mother Bessie Lee Hart Kees Tucker for her endless love, support and understanding. For always encouraging me to go forward until I reach my goals. Nothing is more precious than having a mother as a friend.

To my children who had to sacrifice me while I worked on this book. Thank you Harold, Avery, Latasha, DarVale and Armina for your unconditional love and support. A million thanks to my twelve grandchildren who seldom saw their grandmother during this venture. To my sisters Gloria, Rose and Anita and my big brother Charlie. Love to all my nieces and nephews. To Verna a special friend and sister who I trust with my life.

To all my family and friends who listened endlessly to my poems. Thank you all for being there for me. Loving thanks to my girlfriend Pat Walker (deceased) I wish she were here to share in my accomplishments. Otis Jones whose love and support is truly real. Stephen Pickett whose love for the arts was instrumental in my going forward. My American Medical Response family who always came to my rescue when my health was in question. To Angelina Martinez my neighbor and friend who wrote a poem called "Time to Get It Done". Angelina words were inspirational and will stay with me all my life. Thanks to her encouraging words I got it done.

A very sincere special thanks to Kim Conley-Winters who brought my heart to life with her creative artistic talents. To Dave Turner who added the beautiful finishing touches to the book cover. To Lily Farmer a long time friend who proofread my manuscript, her patience is greatly appreciated. To Past President William Jefferson Clinton for his encouraging letter in acknowledgment of the poem written for him. Thank you all for being a friend.

I believe God put all these special people in my life to bring me happiness where there was sadness. Love where there was pain and fulfillness where there was emptiness. I love you all.

                                                    Shirley A. Jackson

PROLOGUE

I woke up one morning and decided I did not want to pass through life silently. I had a lot of emotions built up inside of me. It took years to realize I was not alone in this world with unconscience pain. I would hear about immoral acts in conversations and the news media, it was never real enough until it hit home.

I never had therapy to deal with all my concealed emotions. After each mind blowing experience I would close a mental door on the pain until it didn't hurt so much. Now I am at the crossroads in my life where I will have to reopen those doors. I must put the past to bed once and for all before I can continue on. I will always carry the scars of my life with the realization that God is my cosmetic surgeon. He took all the ugliness in my life, replanted it in good soil so that I can grow new roots. I am learning that wisdom comes with having a beautiful mind along with a loving and forgiving heart.

This book is the first step in letting go of suppressed feelings through my poetry. God help me as I venture on to unlock the mental doors I fear most. Maybe when its all over I will be able to make sense of all the pain. Maybe I will finally understand why.

Biography

Shirley A. Jackson was born at General Hospital in Los Angeles, California in 1948. The second daughter to Rayfield and Bessie Tucker. Shirley has three sisters Gloria, Rose and Anita. Two brothers Charles and Rayfield Tucker.

After her parents separated they were forced to moved to Imperial Courts projects in Watts, California where she attended Markham Jr. High School. Her mother's financial struggles were overbearing after the separation. Shirley went to live with her father in Fairbanks, Alaska. That's when Shirley's life changed forever. After an unbearable reunion with her father she returned home to her mother in Los Angeles, California.

Shirley married her childhood sweetheart after high school. She now has five children; two daughters LaTasha and Armina. Three sons, Harold, Avery and DarVale. After marital problems she moved to Richmond, California to continue her education at Contra Costa College. Upon completing the general business course at Contra Costa she went into the word processing program at Merritt College in Oakland. Upon moving to San Jose she continued her education at Mission College in Santa Clara. She went on to West Valley College for their small business course. Upon completing the small business course she started a small income tax service.

Upon raising her children she decided to pursue her dream of becoming a writer. Her love of poetry was her inspiration. In July of 1995 she wrote a poem called "Mr. President". This poem was dedicated to President Bill Clinton. On September 7, 1995 she decided to send it to him. October 3, 1995 President Clinton wrote her a letter thanking her for sharing the poem with him.

Her first collection of poems was copywritten under the title "Innersanction, Memoirs through Poetry". "Desensitized Minds" a poem geared to recapture our youth in trouble was published in City Flight Magazine under Street Poetry. To her amazement she was featured on the same page with an article about her best friend's son Andre Young. Becoming a contributing writer to this magazine gave her the boost she needed to keep going after her dream. In 1998 a country western singer (Bryan Jon) ask her to write lyrics for his upcoming album. The first song lyrics written are titled "Hanging Up My Hat". The second song lyrics written is titled "Cowboy Without a Song". Her words never stop flowing and her pen never runs out of ink.

Shirley currently lives in San Jose, California where she enjoys reading poetry and working in her flower garden.

TABLE OF CONTENTS

I. **SPIRITUAL**
   A Prayer For My Children... 14
   A Star In The Night.. 15
   All I have To Give Is Me... 16
   Before I Say Good-by... 17
   Father Remember Me... 139
   From Fertile Ground... 18
   Guardian Angel... 19
   I'm Just Passing Through... 20
   I Wonder.. 152
   It's Christmas Again... 21
   Lord Lift Me Up.. 22
   Mysterious Ways.. 23
   Naked... 27
   No Longer Under Attack... 143
   Now That You've Gone On Ahead.. 25
   Temptations of the Flesh... 13
   Through The Greatness Of His Love.. 26
   Today I Cried... 145
   Voices In The Wind.. 24
   When I Come To Pray.. 28
   When I See God... 148
   When the Walls Come Tumbling Down................................... 29
   You Can't Disassemble My Soul.. 30

II. **FAMILY**
   Always Loving You Dad... 35
   Bessie Lee.. 36
   DaShawn... 33
   Family... 32
   Farewell to A Friend... 40
   Father's Day... 41
   Mama.. 37
   Mama It's Time to Rest.. 38
   Mother's Day.. 39
   Remembering You Daughter.. 42
   Soldier In My Heart.. 34
   The Beauty of You.. 146

TABLE OF CONTENTS

III. LOVE

Anniversary	44
Always Looking Away	45
Anonymous Love	46
Broken Heart Blues	144
Cowboy Without a Song	47
Dancing On Every Star	48
Darryl	49
Deep Penetration	50
Don't Make Me Pay	51
Fairy Tale Lover	52
Falling Petals	53
Finishing Touch	54
First Love	55
Give Me Back My Heart	56
Guilty Three Strikes I'm Out	57
Hickory	58
I Don't Know How to Stop Loving You	59
I Had to Leave My Heart Behind	140
I Keep Seeing You	60
I Knew I Could Love Again	61
I Only Had One Night	64
If Only I Told You I Care	65
I'm Hanging Up My Hat	62
Incarcerated Love	63
Looking For My Love	67
Love Don't Make Sense	66
Loving Online	69
Loving You Hurts	68
My Marriage Vows	70
No Strings Attached	71
Outbreak Of Memories	72
Shake Me Down	73
Today We Wed	74
We Could Have Made it Work	147
When All Time Stopped	75
When You Realized You Need Me	76
When the Past Comes Back	77
Why Did You Take My Love If You Didn't Know What To Do With It	78
Wind Carry My Love Home	79
You Couldn't See For Looking	80

TABLE OF CONTENTS

- IV. FANTASY
  - A Face in the Crowd.. 82
  - Day Dreams.. 83
  - Forbidden Lover... 84
  - I Want An Old Fashion Man.. 86
  - Intimate Moments In My Mind... 85
  - Much Right Man.. 87
  - My Enchanting Sea... 88
  - My Little White House.. 142
  - My Valentine.. 89
  - Parakeet Sing For Me... 90
  - Poet's Dream.. 91
  - Songwriter.. 92
  - Stage Fright.. 93
  - The Artist.. 94
  - The Wind.. 95
  - Tick Tock... 96
  - Wind Chimes.. 97
  - Without Dreams... 98

- V. CELEBRITY
  - Cuong Phu Tran... 100
  - Maya Angelou.. 101
  - Oprah Winfrey.. 102
  - Paravotti.. 104
  - Ten Decades... 103

- VI. SPORTS
  - Football.. 106

- VII. EMOTIONS
  - A Million Can Win... 108
  - Affirmative Action.. 109
  - Am I Sane... 110
  - Andrew Its Time to Rest.. 137
  - Back From Decension.. 111
  - Black Like Me... 114
  - Bond of the Hood.. 138
  - Daddy Don't.. 115
  - Desensitized Minds... 116
  - Distant Dads... 117

TABLE OF CONTENTS

VII. EMOTIONS (Continued)

    Drugs, Tobacco and Alcohol.. 118
    I Am Who I Believe I Am.. 113
    I Am Woman.. 155
    I Don't Wanna Be Carjacked... 119
    It All Starts With You... 153
    Let My People Go.. 120
    Living In The Realm of Abuse... 121
    Mama You're Finally Free.. 141
    March of Kings.. 123
    Martin Luther King.. 124
    Mr. President.. 125
    My Diary... 122
    My Journey... 135
    My Journey (Continued)... 136
    My Little White House... 142
    New Year's Day... 126
    Plight of the Homeless.. 127
    Prejudice... 128
    Prejudice The Demon.. 129
    Reflections... 151
    Rodd.. 154
    Saddle Tramp... 112
    Song Of The Survivors... 130
    The Hills of San Jose.. 131
    This May Be The Last Time.. 132
    Today I Cried.. 148
    When You Can't Turn Life Around....................................... 133
    When You Look at Me Daddy... 149
    When You're a Child.. 150
    Where Do I Draw the Line... 139

PREFACE

I woke up one morning and decided I did not want to pass through life silently. I had a lot of emotions built up inside of me. Inside My Soul is an outpour of emotions. Some of my emotions have been suppressed over the years because I was unable to cope with them. After each heartbreak or disappointment I somehow managed to bounce back convincing myself I must go on no matter what.

I never had professional therapy to deal with my emotions, after each bad experience I would mentally close the door on that incident. Now I am at a crossroads in my life where I will have to reopen those doors, put the past to bed before I can continue on.

I found myself looking for love in all the wrong places hoping for a quick fix to the emptiness in my life. I discovered I was a hopeless romantic and realized I had to focus on what was real and what was pure fantasy.

Inside My Soul is the first step in letting go of my suppressed feelings. God help me as I venture to unlock the doors I fear most. Maybe when it's all over I will understand why.

The hardest thing I ever had to face was the deception from the ones closest to me. I never recovered from pain I just buried it deep inside me. How can you erase the scars that family inflicts? Nothing else in the world can cut so deep. It took years to realize I was not alone in this world and it was not my fault. I would hear about immoral acts in the news but it was never real enough until it hit home.

I believe God sent a guardian angel to watch over me and my family and to keep me safe. Motherhood has been my greatest challenge. The love of my children is what keeps me going.

Why I Write

I am concerned about malicious acts in the night,
if I can change someone's vicious thoughts, this is why I write.

I see countless people in need barely surviving their endless plight,
if I can help turn their world around, this is why I write,

One day someone will finally hear my pleas and make things right,
the powers that be might listen to reason, this is why I write.

When I touch someone with my words my heart takes flight,
if I can bring a little comfort to someone's life, this is why I write.

When I close my eyes at night I know someone's child is alright,
inside my words someone will heard my cries, this is why I write,

If I can help someone in trouble to stop running for their life,
by guiding them to a safe haven today, this is why I write.

I won't take up arms against my brother, this is how I choose to fight,
my pen is my power, my words are my strength, this is why I write.

Shirley A. Jackson

SPIRITUAL

Temptations of the Flesh

Mind over matter is what some people believe.
If true why can't I make these nasty little demons leave.

When I try to turn my life around they knock me to the ground.
I keep getting back up I won't let them hold me down.

Everyday they plot against me just to have some fun.
One day the power of my faith will have them on the run.

Father please walk along side me guiding every step I make.
I give my soul only to you Father, my demons cannot take.

You gave me the insight of knowing right from wrong.
I've struggled with temptations for so very long.

You said man should not be alone, from his rib came his mate.
Will my mate come with your blessings, I will continue to wait?

I made numerous mistakes blinded by sins along the way.
I've chosen the path of righteousness; this is where I'll stay.

Hold on to me Father don't allow them to pull me away.
Everyday is a tug of war with my demons don't let me stray.

These horrid little demons won't give my soul a rest.
They're always taunting me with temptations of the flesh.

A Prayer For My Children

I am troubled about my children growing up in a world with misguided morals.
I tried to prepare them for today's society; Lord help me show them the way.

Guide my children through this maze of demons that are here to stay.
They will have your love as a guiding light as you cast all the demons away.

Now that I look back on my life I can see where I made some mistakes.
I made it through trouble water Lord, my children lives were at stake.

You have blessed me thus far with healthy infants now grown to adulthood.
I tried to reinforce your presence in their lives; I hope they all understood.

My children are trying so hard to achieve goals and to find their own way.
Peer pressure, temptations and prejudice is trying to lead them astray.

They are constantly looking for some place where they can all fit in.
Family ties are not strong as they should be, there is no help from next of kin.

I did not have all the answers they were looking for; I shared everything I knew.
I always remind them life would be real tough Lord if they live it without you.

My children were fruitful; they all have mates and their own children to.
Will you watch over my grandchildren; they need your help to make it through.

I can remember when I could not wait until they all had left home.
I did not realize how empty my home would be when they were all gone.

I sent my children into the world armed with love so their adult life could begin.
I pray I will be by your side in Heaven Lord when they all come home again.

This is a troubled mother's prayer; I turn to you Lord in my moment of despair.
I was taught by my mother to bring all my troubles to you Lord in prayer.

Show them the path of righteous, in you Lord they can truly win.
Please accept this prayer from me Lord; this is a prayer for my children.

A Star In The Night

I stood outside in the midnight hour letting the night winds caress me.
I watched rain clouds blanketing the sky moving westward running free.

As the clouds passed I saw an opening with a bright star shining through.
I marveled at the lights dancing in the heavens; all of a sudden I knew.

The clearing in the sky this December night is a remainder of our Lord's birth.
This is a time for all mankind to join in together to achieve peace on earth.

This is a time when we must look a lot deeper into our hearts.
No matter how big or small our contribution we can give someone a new start.

Magnificent star so near, yet so far shining so bright.
I envision blessings gliding down your rays camouflaged by lights.

Our father keeps sending blessings; we must be doing something right.
Guide me with wisdom, love and compassion whenever I see a star in the night.

All I Have To Give Is Me

When I was driving home today I wanted to thank God in my own special way.

I wanted to thank him for my life; my salvation and the son he gave away.

I wanted to do something different not like anyone else.

Alters have been built, songs have been sung, stories have been written and candles burnt on a shelf.

What can I do Lord so when you look down I will stand out from all the rest.

I don't know if I have the patience of Job; can I possibly survive that test.

Do I have the faith of John the Baptist who loved you until the bitter end?

Lord do I have the true spirit of your followers who witnessed you rise again.

Lord everything down here is nothing but material things.

Other than loving you I don't know how else I can earn my wings.

After hours of thinking about a special gift it finally hit me; why did it take so long for me to see?

I wasted my time looking elsewhere I had the gift all along, all I have to give is me.

Before I Say Good-by

Sometimes I may have appeared to be kind of tough.
I tried to prepare you for the real world; people play pretty rough.

I tried to protect you from people who didn't have your interest at heart.
I wanted to educate you early so you would have a good start.

I did everything I knew how to give you a good home life.
One that was free from drinking, drugs and family fights.

The problems never stopped; I didn't know where they all came from.
I didn't have all the answers to all our problems I took them on one by one.

Each one of you had your own individual personalities.
No matter what you did you all managed to get a smile out of me.

All of you have your own special place in my heart.
We are all bound by our love for each other; never let anyone tear that apart.

Look out for one another life is so short you only get one chance.
Don't let a worthless feeling like jealousy interfere and take its stance.

Remember family is everything; family will always be there for you.
Try to include your family in everything that you do.

My sons stand tall, love and protect your families you can't go wrong.
My daughters stand behind your man and help him to be strong.

I pray that God keep you all safe from harm and all of you have a good life.
It all starts at home with love and family, your husband and your wife.

When times get tough don't fight try praying and holding on to each other.
Families that pray together stay together; for once listen to your mother.

When things get tough and you need support just turn your heads to the sky.
I want you all to know how much I really love you before I say good-by.

From Fertile Ground

I am thankful to you Lord for giving me the gift of motherhood,
the responsibilities that came with this gift were clearly understood.

When the seeds of life were planted in my fertile womb,
the transformation into motherhood didn't come a moment too soon.

I didn't really know how precious life was until I gave birth,
in the mist of uncertain times there are still miracles here on earth.

Trying to do the right thing for my children made motherhood real tough.
I kept my faith through it all Lord, especially when things got a little rough.

It hurts when a family member is taken away and we have to say good-by,
love is the family strength not even death can break those ties.

Lord you sacrificed your son for our sins allowing our lives to continue,
now I raise my children in your name Lord, I'm giving them back to you.

I've explored the history of life from the books of Genesis through Revelations,
it saddens my heart Lord to see diminishing family relations?

A mother's prayer is to live long enough to raise her children and set them free,
unworthy that I am Lord thank you for listening to me.

I am truly blessed to have my children and grandchildren around,
when I first conceived I could not imagine what would grow from fertile ground.

Guardian Angel

Every morning when I wake up, I thank God in my own personal way,
I thank God for his blessings and letting me see another day.

I understand the meaning of "Behold I stand at the door and knock",
I opened up that door a long time ago so he can come into my heart.

Sometimes voices try to lead me astray and it gives me such a fright,
I am not sure that everything I am doing is completely right.

I find myself on a path of mental and physical self-destruction,
before it gets completely out of hand I'm turned in another direction.

Every time I find myself distraught or caught in a life threatening situation,
something strange always happens to end the altercation.

Sometime life comes down on me so hard I start hyperventilating,
my Angel brings me up for air preparing me for what's waiting.

When I find myself in harm's way and someone's going to hurt me,
my Guardian Angel reaches out and pulls me back to safety.

My children and grandchildren, live far away from home,
my Angel eases my fears by assuring me they too don't walk alone.

As I progress through age I see things a lot differently,
I believe I have a purpose, I wonder what God has in store for me.

Every time I try to rebel against my faith and get on a fast track,
I can feel that Guardian Angel of mine pulling me right back.

I'm Just Passing Through

I must travel this journey walking through fruitless land,
when my shadow passes over me, he will extend his hand.

After the sacrifice he made I will bask in his glory,
as long as I stay on the straight and narrow path I will have no worry.

The road home will be a long challenging one,
when I see the city paved in gold I know I will have won.

I will pick up knowledge and wisdom along the way,
when I retire in my father's kingdom it will be a glorious day.

I've built an altar in my heart so I will never stray,
I bring my all to the altar when I come to pray.

Accept my home coming Lord, your imperfect child,
I will praise thy name while I walk this endless mile.

Life may taunt or tempt me with its insufferable sins,
my fortitude is my belief that I hold within.

Evil always test my faith during the dark hours of night,
little do they know long ago I had seen the light.

I won't turn my soul inside out just to appease you,
I'm looking towards higher ground; I'm just passing through.

It's Christmas Again,

This is the season I honor my lord and savior and praise his holy name.
Life as we knew it changed forever on the blessed night that he came.

He brought with him forgiveness, love, faith and a path that leads to home.
He made us fishers of men to spread the gospel so we won't aimlessly roam.

Every year this time people run around trying to find gifts to say I love you.
I've learned that love shows in all the little things that you do.

It's not expensive gifts, fabulous vacations, new homes or flashy cars.
Just a walk, holding hands, gentle kisses under a night sky filled with stars.

I love the history our ancestors created, but I don't want to live in the past.
Living in the here and now I want a relationship that is going to last.

The future although full of mysteries I truly look forward to.
If I were blessed with a future I would like to share my adventures with you.

My prayer is my Heavenly Father keeps your family prosperous and safe.
Share your blessings with the sick and needy whose lives are at stake.

I pray the coming years are filled with great tidings and good cheers.
It's Christmas again my friend, Season's Greetings and a Happy New Year.

Lord Lift Me Up

Lord lift me up,
my burdens are weighing me down.
Life is holding me for ransom,
I can't keep my feet on the ground.

Lately I feel like I'm on a dead-end street
living in this crazy mixed up town.
The only way I can get through this maze
is knowing you're always around.

The evils in this world
are always running about.
Sometime I get so full inside
it makes me want to shout.

Send the winds Lord
to carry my troubles away.
When I open my eyes again
I want to see a clearer day.

Just like my Lord did years passed
I carry my cross on my back.
I will always praise your name my Lord,
especially when I am under attack.

When life takes its toll on me
and times start to get real tough,
I raise my hands in the air
and cry Lord lift me up.

Mysterious Ways

Lord I praise you and thank you for allowing me to see another day.
Living the way I do I am unworthy of your blessings but you give them anyway.

Unclean spirits enter my weak mind convincing me to give in without a fight.
I turn away ashamed of my actions; through you Lord I can make things right.

I pray for guidance this world is so confusing, I don't know where to begin.
I accept you as my savior Lord; I don't want to give into unclean spirits again.

Will I always have this battle within myself until I am laid down to rest.
Whatever path I must take I will endure because you know what's best.

I've had many disappointments my heart hardened, my feelings are suppressed.
Turning the other cheek is so hard Lord it has caused me so much stress.

Its almost impossible to find someone you can trust down here they are so rare.
I haven't given up yet; I have to believe you won't give me more than I can bear.

When I make a bad decision taking a path that leads to a dead end.
A solution to all my problems appear and the blessings start coming again.

Through it all Lord I knew once you entered my heart you were here to stay.
I don't have the answers all I know is Lord you have some mysterious ways.

Naked

The commandments I am governed by were slowly vanishing,
I was molested by evil itself trying to change my way of believing.

My mind had been raped by a deceitful and immoral society,
polluted thoughts were trying to take control of me.

I was once wrapped in clean cloth washed in the Holy Spirit,
I watched my cloth loosen at the seams and did not try mend it.

My cloth fell from my shoulders exposing my nakedness,
evil spirits covered me in soiled clothing before I knew it.

How did I let my eyes become blind to all the impure acts?
My shepherd always go after his stray lambs to bring them all back.

My foundation never crumpled beneath me; it was built on solid ground,
when I thought my soul was lost I realized I had been found.

My soiled cloth was washed clean with love and forgiveness,
having a forgiving God is to understand his greatness.

My faith will hold steadfast, I know I am going to make it,
never again in my lifetime will I get caught naked.

Now That You've Gone On Ahead

We are now separated only for a very little while.
Until we are reunited again I'll always remember your smile.

Sharing my life with you has always been my first choice.
In the whispers of the winds I will remember your precious voice.

I will cherish all the memories of your thoughtful and unselfish ways.
Tender loving thoughts of you will surely fill my empty days.

I will have you in my thoughts daily when I go for a quiet walk.
I will forever have your understanding when I need to have a talk.

You may not be where my eyes can clearly see,
I know within my heart you'll always be watching over me.

When I see the stars twinkling I know you are watching from above.
Send a shooting star my way in remembrance of our love.

Your love I can hold on to eternally, it will never fade away,
When we became one and bonded our love was here to stay.

I will keep you in my prayers every night before I go to bed.
Prepare a place for our reunion now that you've gone on ahead.

Written for Paramedic Cheeseman my co-worker who came home from work to find her young husband had passed in his sleep one afternoon.

Through The Greatness of Your Love

Through the greatness of your love I find peace,
from my waking hours
until I fall sound asleep.

Through the greatness of your love I have hope,
I see a world with no wars,
people loving one another,
no children tormented by dope.

Through the greatness of your love I find caring,
no more selfish acts,
families supporting each other,
people giving cheerfully, always sharing.

Through the greatness of your love,
I know the promises made you will keep,
until my soul arrives in your kingdom
my heart will continue to weep.

Every time I see a rainbow hovering above,
it reminds me that my life was created
through the greatness of your love.

Voices In The Wind

When I hear the wind whistling through my window panes,
I wonder if it came alone or if it brought some rain.

I love to walk quietly in my thoughts on a windy day,
I don't run from it when it surrounds me, I let it have its way.

Days when my spirits are down thinking about love ones passed on,
I can hear a chorus of voices in the wind, singing a beautiful song.

They tell me to hold on to my faith, God knows my pain, and it won't be long,
God's love is not measured by our time, they will see me when I get home.

When job stress, finances, family and friends get the best of me,
I turn to the voices in the wind for comfort, they open my eyes so I can see.

Sometime it feels like I'm a boxer fighting life in the fifteenth round,
each time life hits me with hard punches, I refuse to let it knock me down.

I hear the wind coming up, time for another walk and rest under the elm tree,
I've just won another title fight with life because God was my referee.

When I see my friends give up on faith, I ask why did you close that gate,
open it back up, God is still there, just be patient, keep your faith and wait.

The wind is blowing gently through my soul; I can hear those voices again,
this time the voices are saying thank you for helping out another friend.

I don't know how to pray like the Lord's disciples passed down through time,
I cast my prayers into the wind to carry home, God knows they are mine.

Accept my prayers Lord; you are my Father, Savior and my spiritual friend.
I am reminded of your love for me every time I hear those voices in the wind.

I wrote this poem when my grandfather passed away. He was eighty-six years young. He was always so proud of my accomplishments. He would brag to everyone who would listen about me. Sometimes he would exaggerate a little. I miss him so much. I needed more time with him. I love you Pops.

When I Come To Pray

What do I pray for Lord in the world today?
When morals, family values, forgiveness has all gone astray.

Children killing, divorcing and abusing their mother and father,
parents discarding their responsibilities, please bring them back to the altar.

Religious leaders turning a deaf ear to their own preaching,
our education system is failing our children with the way they are teaching.

Racism and hate crimes growing at an alarming rate,
no matter where you attempt to go there is no way to escape.

Everyday people are terminating their precious lives,
what's more disheartening is a gifted physician's assisted suicide.

Although I am detained in this valley of death with no where to hide,
I am thankful for your blessings when you walk by my side.

The strength I draw from your love takes some of my pain away,
I carry all the sins of the world with me Lord when I come to pray.

When The Walls Come Tumbling Down

Little demons out of hell I won't let you toy with me in my finest hour,
if I give into you even for a second it'll extend your ugly powers.

In the pits of my hollow sour stomach is where you wade,
one day at a time with each battle I win I'll watch your powers fade.

If I lose a battle in my mind it will surely affect my mental health,
with each battle won I am showered in blessings of endless wealth.

You deceived me unexpectedly with the vicious gift of your Trojan horse,
I will not let these spiteful little demons once inside run their course.

When it gets so tough I can't find strength to get up out of my chair,
I believe in my heart my troubles won't be more than I can bear.

I'm going into battle with my golden shield of faith and sword in my hand,
trusting in the promises of my Savior this is where I take my stand.

When life's obstacles test my faith I won't bow my head to the ground,
I'll hold my head up high towards Heaven when the walls come tumbling down.

You Can't Disassemble My Soul

I went to see my family physician for an examination and tests.
I am concerned about my body not being able to handle the stress.

He referred me to a specialist whom he felt was one of the best.
My doctor was concerned about a lump he felt inside my breasts.

His words burned deep in my mind; this is every woman's fear.
The thought of losing my breasts had me on the brink of tears.

Woman is one of God's beautiful and well-defined creatures.
It's disheartening to think that I could lose my attractive features.

I survived thus far on my faith alone; I'll wait to see what the tests reveal.
If it comes back positive I'll still trust in God, I know that he can heal.

I am not going to get depressed and fall into an emotional slump.
I pray that God guide the surgeon's hands when he removes that lump.

I knew I would have to leave my body behind someday right from the start.
My body houses my soul temporarily but I would like to keep all my parts.

With each operation I feel like I'm being disassembled as I grow old.
As long as my spiritual life is right it's not important if my body is not whole.

The Lord is my shepherd I shall not weep; I learned this a long time ago.
You may alter my physical being but you can't disassemble my soul.

FAMILY

Family

You were family when you exited your mother's womb.
You will always be family from the womb to the tomb.

When you feel like you are drifting away hold out a hand.
Family comes together when needed and take a loving stand.

The strength of family is so strong it will never let you get away.
The love will bring you back no matter how far or how long you stray.

Society sometimes traps you into believing your family is thugs or drugs.
Family won't turn their back on you; they restrain, its called tough love.

When you're feeling low there is something you should know.
No matter who try to come between us family won't ever let go.

When things seem uncertain and your mind creates unwanted fears.
Reach out for your family, the love only grows stronger over the years.

Our greatest trials are when we lose love ones to inevitable death.
This is the time when family comes together before the final rest.

Its exciting to witness what the combined knowledge of family creates.
Family rejoices in the achievements of loves ones, that when we celebrate.

God first was embedded in our souls through our ancestor's bloodline.
Take God with you everywhere you go, don't ever leave God behind.

Our family tree has many branches that extend farther than the eye can see.
There is nothing more important in life than keeping together the family.

DaShawn

To my voyager who gives of himself,
away from love ones trying to help.
Many miles away from home,
occasional letter, very little phone.

New challenges have you wayward bound,
never knowing where you will be found.
Very little laughter in the air,
only because you are no longer there.

My little child now grown up into a man,
giving of himself doing the best he can.
I'm dragging my heart on the cold floor,
waiting for you to come though the door.

Stand tall my child don't ever stray,
let them know you are here to stay.
Your heart is big as you are brave.
Keep your faith until you enter your grave.

We are under the same sky of blue,
remember always I truly love you.
I love you today and more tomorrow,
I think of you with love never sorrow.

Listen to the eternal beat of your heart,
once you're home we will never part.
My tears are filled with pain and joy,
I wait for your return, my soldier boy.

Written for my nephew DaShawn Rachel who went honorably to serve his country. I use to take care of him. Now he watches over me.

Soldier In My Heart

I know you have to do what you feel is right,
your sacrifices is what allow people to fall asleep at night.

You went away to join a team that would make you proud,
I bet you never imagine screams in the night would be so loud.

When people cry for help you're willing to give a helping hand,
feelings run deep as we watch you leave for a foreign land.

You accept the challenge not knowing what lies ahead,
the only consolation is your family is safe at home in bed.

Your courage and devotion will be handed down to your heirs,
I pray for more peaceful solutions to all of our foreign affairs.

Sometimes we pay a high cost for the freedom we share,
never doubt our gratitude for a moment that you are there.

Every day you are on watch you're saving someone's life,
in God we trust you'll make it through another day without a fight.

Bloodstains with honor are in the stripes of our red, white and blue,
pride, faith and belief is the instinctive force that truly drives you.

The day will come when you no longer will have to roam,
I will be here waiting with open arms when you finally return home.

The thing I hate most is your orders always make us part,
just close your eyes to feel my love soldier in my heart.

This poem was written for my nephew DaShawn Rachel when we feared his orders would take him to Afghanistan after the World Trade Center came down on 9/11.

Always Loving You Dad

A tower of strength, you are such an illustrious man,
as a child I loved walking with you while holding your hand.

I want to thank you for giving me so much quality time,
I was always proud to let everyone know that this dad was mine.

I watched you work hard, you were always willing and able,
no matter how times were you manage to put food on our table.

It wasn't easy but we made it through some stormy weathers,
no matter what happened you always kept the family together.

I know we had our little disagreements and my childish fights,
you still accepted the choices I made and kept me a part of your life.

You built a strong foundation for me to grow from and kept me on track,
when I left home you kept the door open for me to always come back.

Decades have passed and seeing you still warms my heart,
you give me strength to survive in this world although we are miles apart.

Nothing in this world can ever break this bond we have,
every time you think of me just remember I'm always loving you Dad.

Written for my friend Treena Johnson for her father to say how much she loved him. Mr. Johnson passed away a year later.

Bessie Lee

Mother I am writing this poem especially for you.
I am expressing my love the only way I know how; every word is absolutely true.

When I was in adolescence I tried to please you by doing my chores.
When I became a teenager and fell in love I didn't listen to you anymore.

I was such a rebellious kid; I couldn't wait to leave home.
After I got a taste of life on the streets I realize my decision was wrong.

I learned quickly that experience is not easy but it is the best teacher.
I should have paid more attention and listen to the words of our preacher.

When I finally settled down, married and had children of my own.
I learned to appreciate you a lot more after my children were all grown.

Mother please forgive me for all the pain I put you through.
Please accept my apology Mom, through it all I never stopped loving you.

Mother I want you to know all your teaching was not in vain.
All the values you've instilled in me while I was young fortunately still remain.

Thank you for your understanding and always being there for me.
I am so proud to be a part of your ever-growing family tree.

I've given you grandchildren who in turn gave you great grandchildren to.
There is so much love coming from this branch and it's all attributed to you.

Mother you've seen and experienced some pretty tough times in the past.
I saw you juggle jobs, children, husbands through bad times that didn't last.

You are a perfect example of how a loving mother should be.
Thank you for opening my eyes making me see;
how blessed I am to have a mother who loves me by the name of Bessie Lee.

Mama

My grandmother is full of life although she is almost a century old,
her knowledge of life in itself is worth its weight in gold.

Every time I would visit I'd ask her to tell me a story,
with each story she told I would learn more about our family history.

Mama is blessed to have the gift of a good memory to take me back in time,
I was intrigued at the stories about bootleggers hiding illegal wine.

Mama spoke of our ancestors in the underground railroad as runaway slaves,
she told of their plight traveling only by night and sleeping by day in cold caves.

Mama always lived by the golden rule,
I love the one about how many miles she had to walk to school.

Mama is a strong believer if you spare the rod you'll spoil the child,
when I did something wrong I could not sit down for a while.

Mama is a strong woman with a whole lot of pride,
she walks with her head held high letting you know she has nothing to hide.

Mama stood by my grandfather for sixty years until God called him home,
she believes God keeps his promises and she will never be alone.

Through it all my grandfather kept his vows not until death did they part,
although his body has returned to the earth his spirit in still in her heart.

I hope someday I will have the strength that she possess,
1 will love you always Mama even after my body is laid to rest.

February 14, 2004 my grandmother who we call Mama Edna (Edna Kees) was 96 years old. I always love to hear stories of her younger days. She is slowly losing her memory. I will miss those old stories.

Mama Its Time to Rest

I knew the day would come when our Lord and Savior would call you home.
I know you are in a better place Mama but I feel so alone.

You did everything in your power to keep our family together.
No matter what happened we made it thorough some stormy weather.

Every new challenge that came along it only made you strong.
You nurtured our family doing everything in your power to make a home.

You planted a lot of seeds in me when I was young and scared.
You put the good book in my hand and said remember the things I've read.

Growing up I know some of my decisions you were not so happy about.
I know you wanted the best for me, it was in your voice even when you shout.

I thank God for letting you see your generations grow and grow.
Every time I see the son of my son I will see all the love that you show.

You gave us your best Mama, now this world has taken its toll on you.
No more pain, sickness, and suffering only a rainbow across a sky of blue.

I see you lying there so peaceful and I'm fighting back the tears in my eyes.
I love you so Mama now the time has come for me to say good-bye.

I know you're in our Father's glorious kingdom; for you surely that's the best.
I'll carry your loving spirit with me always, now Mama its time to rest.

One of my closest friends lost her grandmother at 89 years young. She was like a grandmother to me also. She welcomed me in her home like I was her own. Her husband now deceased as well would come on Sunday mornings to take my children to Sunday school. Mr. and Mrs. Dixon were wonderful people. This was a great loss. I read this poem at Mrs. Dixon's funeral.

Mother's Day

Mother's Day is a day set aside especially for mothers like you,
it's a day to express one's love and to thank you for all that you do.

There's is no wages for this job entitled motherhood it's all volunteer,
recognition for a job well done comes around year after year.

You'll be remembered for all the times that your children became ill,
being there in a crisis while holding on to a strong will.

Your children look up to you for your knowledge, strength and wisdom,
it's not an easy thing to try and make all the right decisions.

All you have to remember is to have their best interest at heart,
show your love in everything you do and you won't ever drift apart.

When your children do something that you don't agreed with,
just remember when you were young and try hard to understand it.

If you build your foundation on faith you can turn to God when they stray,
let God handle it when the time comes for your children to go away.

Every time I think about you daughter it gives me a happy heart,
our love was not developed over the years it was always there from the start.

I can still remember clearly when you were my beautiful baby girl,
the sparkle in your eyes, your bright smile and your little head full of curls.

The miles separate us physically but you hold my heart in your hand,
during our separation hold on to my loving thoughts for as long as you can.

On this designated day I want to say I love you in a very special way,
this poem was written especially for you my daughter to celebrate Mother's Day.

I wrote this poem especially for my two beautiful daughters who are loving mothers themselves. My daughters not only grew into good courageous women they became my best friends. I love you both more than anything in this world LaTasha and Armina. Mom

Farewell To A Friend

We have share each other's lives for so many years,
we've shared triumphs, defeats, good times and shed many tears.

We shared money between us when things got a little tight,
we always found a way to forgive each other after our silly little fights.

When we were young we lived our lives to the fullest,
when we got older we learn we could be happy with a little less.

The past few years has taken its toll on our matured bodies,
we walk slower, hearing is fading, need bifocals to help us see.

We walked a many miles together and survived a rugged sea,
every time the smoke finally cleared it's always been you and me.

We worried many days whether or not our children chose the right path,
we gave it our best shot now our children have to clean up their act.

You are my confidant, and closer to me than my next of kin,
I can turn to you for anything because you are my closest friend.

Every time I hear a foghorn or see a school of scurrying fish,
I'll remember your love for fishing, you will surly be missed.

I've shed my tears, addressed my pain, not holding anything within,
Now as much as I love you I must say farewell to a friend.

This poem was written for my best friend Patsy Walker. We had a lot of good times together. We talked on the telephone two or three times everyday. Our husbands thought we were strange. We were just like sisters with unconditional love. She had a mouth like a sailor. God I miss her.

Father's Day

Today is a special day to commemorate only you,
A special day to remember all the good things that you do.

A time to say thank you for all the quality time we share.
A time to remember you showing me how much you really care.

A time to appreciate how you made me play by all the rules.
A time to understand why you wanted me to always do well in school.

A time to remember how you made me face all my fears.
A time to remember when you would wipe away my running tears.

A time to remember the discipline you enforced whenever I was bad.
A time to remember how you brighten up my day whenever I was sad.

A time to remember how you taught me to stand up for my rights.
A time to remember your words "don't give up without a fight."

A time to remember how you always stood so proud and tall.
A time to remember that you'll be there for me if ever I shall fall.

A time to remember how you stood by me whenever I doubted myself.
A time to remember the helping hand you gave whenever I needed help.

A time to remember how you worked so hard to give me a good home.
All through my emotional changes you would remind me I was never alone.

I am proud to have you father, my love for you will never fade away.
This is why I am showering you with my love on this special Father's Day.

To my grandfather William Kees. For all the love he showed over the years. Now that he is gone I have the memories to keep me strong. I thank God for the time we had together.

Remembering You Daughter

When you were developing inside my womb,
I would rock you softly and hum you a little tune.

As you grew inside me while growing your hair,
I had my way of letting you know that I really care.

The day you were born I knew you were mine to keep,
I remember counting the number of toes on your little feet.

Do you remember the warmth, and milk from my breast,
my smiling eyes looking at you snuggled in my caress.

Your terrible two years really put my patience to the test,
especially when you turned the house into a big mess.

Your unperfected teenage years was my biggest concern,
I had some emotional trauma, but you had to learn.

No matter what type of changes I put you through,
your love for me never stopped, this I always knew.

We still have so many years ahead to be together,
even if I have to share you with sisters or brothers.

There are so many things daughter I really want to say,
I want to express my love always, not just on Mother's day.

In my life please know there could never be another,
whenever I think of love I am remembering you daughter.

To LaTasha and Armina, with love. Mom

LOVE

ANNIVERSARY

This is the day I look forward to every year.
The time when we celebrate the love we hold so dear.

All the memories we share all come rushing back.
We survived all our obstacles and kept our marriage in tact.

During the good times and bad times we never drifted apart.
On this special day every year for us it means a brand new start.

Together we created new lives and watched our children grow.
A strong foundation is where our children found their strength I know.

As our seeds are carried forward into our future generations,
our love will go with them as they become part of our great nation.

We did not have all the answers to our problems when they did arise.
We made it though all our trials because you stayed here by my side.

I want this day to always remain sacred and to us hold true.
Today is a confirmation of how much I really do need and love you.

Take a deep breath then exhale my darling, this is no time to get weary.
In twelve short months ahead we'll have another Anniversary.

Always Looking Away

You pace back and forth when you're home restless as can be.
There's not enough excitement being home with the kids and me.

I guess the honeymoon is over and reality is finally setting in.
You're still looking for something it's so obvious you can't pretend.

I can't believe that you want to have your cake and eat it all too.
I can't ignore your actions; time will come when you have to choose.

Just remember when you make your choice, someone else has to lose.
You made your own bed baby remember it won't be me that you use.

Do you know what you want? Are you looking for someone new?
Right now you've got me heart broken and down right blue.

I won't keep crying night after night under a blue moon.
I hope you find what you're looking for honey real soon.

I don know how I will survive without you but I will have to try.
How do we explain to the kids it's time to say good-by?

You still have itchy feet and a mad thirst I guess inside I always knew.
If you leave me don't look back cause I won't be here waiting for you.

Anytime you dance to the music some day you will have to pay.
You can't appreciate the good thing you have: you're always looking away.

Anonymous Love

I run into you from time to time.
Hoping someday you will be mine.

You walk by me so gracefully.
I can bet you don't even notice me.

I can't find the nerve to ask your name.
It feels like I'm playing the hide and seek game.

I'm like the unknown artist who won't reveal himself.
I don't want you to think that mentally I need help.

I wonder what type of person you really want in your life.
I can give you whatever it takes to make things right.

I hesitate approaching you; I guess I'm afraid of rejection.
I can imagine how many people are competing for your affection.

When I close my eyes at night I see you walking with me in my dreams.
I wake up the next morning wondering what it all means.

I want to walk with you during a midnight rain.
My feelings for you are all bundled up; linked like chains.

The only thing more sobering than crickets singing in the night.
Is your breathtaking smile shown by candlelight.

What I'm feeling for you is real; it's not just simple lust.
I can't love you from a distance; I don't want to remain anonymous.

Cowboy without a Song

Like a crazy bull I thought I would play in greener pastures.
Fool that I am, I didn't think about what would happen after.

I made a vow of devotion while breaking every rule.
I never knew that in your worst hour you could be so cruel.

I am sitting here alone thinking around a campfire light.
Wondering who is the stranger making love to my wife.

I can't stand being out here without you all alone.
Knowing you were enjoying him in our home.

What went wrong with our love? Why did we fight?
Now when I see the kids I need visitation rights.

I saw you with him smiling and making plans.
If you turn around and look you'll see a broken man.

I ask the man upstairs to help me cause my heart is in danger.
I'm on that lonesome road again feeling like the lone ranger.

I am the one that really loves you; I can't break your hold.
Do you still love me a little or has your heart grown cold?

I cannot take back what happened, I am the blame.
The feelings that I have for you remain unchanged.

You are the rhythm in my heart and the melody in my soul.
Your words are the lyrics in my mind speaking so bold.

Can't you forgive me I know what I did was wrong.
Now that you left me I am a cowboy without a song.

DANCING ON EVERY STAR

I built my whole world all around you,
I trust my feelings; one look in your eyes and I knew.

Every day we wake up together our love will be brand new,
my heart added another beat; now it beats for two.

We're bonded for life in our eternal love,
my heart leaps through the unconquered galaxy above.

Our love defy gravity as it reaches beyond this planet,
we generate more excitement than Haley's comet.

When you see a shooting star light up the night sky,
it's a tribute to our undying love as it passes by.

Star of my love, star of my heart,
we revolve around each other never apart.

Shine on our devotion, shine in our thoughts,
let your love light shine in our hearts.

Behold the eastern galaxy these are the stars I saw first,
the twinkling of every star is spreading our love throughout the universe.

Imagine our love beyond earthly boundaries; clear pass Mars,
can you see the trail our love left behind while dancing on every star?

Darryl

I once met a tall, dark and handsome man,
who I welcomed in my home with an open heart and hands.
He came to me with a heavy heart and troubles on his back,
all resulting from the constant use of crack.

My mind warned me to turn him away,
but my heart lost control and it ran astray.
I pride myself in being smart and strong,
But once in his arms it didn't last to long.

I always held a fantasy like in the movie 9½ Weeks,
I never knew I was playing this game for keeps.
He separated me from some of my prize possessions,
and destroyed my trust and feelings after his confession.

His illness led him to a long incarceration,
where his freedom was taken without consideration.
He's now looking back on his life with a lot of remorse,
now with the 3 Strikes Law he is not given a choice.

He uses his charm to try and control my life,
then refuses to give up without a fight.
I have to ignore my feelings and find my own way,
I must leave his fate to God, so every night I pray.

When my prayers are answered, and my spiritual life is in tact,
I'll look back remembering the day, God rid the world of Crack.

Deep Penetration

I can feel the need for your loving, my mind is all hazy,
hurry home to me soon lover before I go crazy.

Thoughts of your silky body is spinning around inside my head,
fantasies are what I cling to for the moment as I lay here in bed.

Where are you lover the minutes seem like hours?
I know once you take me in your arms the night will become ours.

I want to kiss you all over, starting from your head down to your feet,
this winter night will feel like summer from all our body heat.

The rain is falling I can hear the drops dancing on the rooftop,
it will enhance our loving, hurry home lover before it stops.

The atmosphere is set with soft music playing in the background,
my heart is filled with excitement racing around and around.

I can feel complete ecstasy erupting inside my every heartbeat;
when our bodies reunite and our souls once again meet.

When I am in your embrace you have total control of my every move,
I feel like a winner crossing the finishing line, I can never lose.

Can I go on like this another day, enslaved by our intimate relations,
when I think I've escaped from your loving I can feel the deep penetration.

Don't Make Me Pay

I understand you had a previous relationship that went sour.
Are you going to make me pay for their mistake hour after hour?

I know you're telling yourself over and over it won't happen again.
It won't happen if you let go of the past and let our future begin.

When will you stop comparing me to your last disappointing mate.
If our relationship is going to survive you have to let go of this hate.

I'm trying to be patient until you find a way to work things out.
I had hoped by now you would have noticed what I'm all about.

Will you ever be strong enough to fight what's been eating at you.
Should I brace myself for the backlash; what am I going to go through?

You're not alone in this self-made hell with feelings you've incarcerated.
When you stop feeling sorry for yourself, look how long I have waited.

Don't lead me on, nothing is worse than being the lover caught on the rebound.
It's time to get your head on straight and plant your feet on solid ground.

Take another look at me, I really do care; look at what you've found.
If you continue to put me on the back burner one day I won't be around.

I'm in your corner for life if you're serious about wanting me.
It's your call lover you can keep this shield around you or set yourself free.

I went into this relationship with my eyes open and I intend to stay.
I'm not the one who took advantage of your love so don't make me pay.

Fairy Tale Lover

You know how to bring out the best in me,
our passion can warm even the coldest seas.

When you take me in your forever welcoming arms,
all my fears are erased, I am safe from all harm.

No one knows me inside and out like you do,
you wake up feelings I've buried only you can see through.

You take our loving every time to brand new heights,
I feel the blood racing through my veins giving me a little fright.

God must have sent you to me only he could have understood,
all I know is that loving you the way I do sure does feel good.

Every night I lay down with you in between soft gentle sheets,
I lose my heart over and over again, its yours to keep.

You know all the right words to say when I need them the most,
when we sit down to dinner in the evening its you I want to toast.

Look me in the eyes and tell me our love is real, it will never die,
I can't live a moment without you, my love for you I cannot hide.

Hold me tight lover I never want the nights to come to an end,
you're my trophy in this game called love, I know I can win.

Your love sedates me, I don't want to wake up in the morning only to discover,
everything was just a dream and you're just a fairy tale lover.

Falling Petals

Our love is like a beautiful red rose.
With the right care our love will grow and grow.

Our love will bloom in any kind of weather.
When new buds appear it will bond us closer together.

The heat we generate is our morning sunshine.
Your eyes are more intoxicating than the finest of wines.

Our love creates music by the light of the moon.
My heart dance with excitement while my pulse swoon.

Gentle kisses on my lips will forever linger.
To warm our winter nights in the midst of December.

When I see a rose petal that has a gentle kiss of dew.
I lose conscience with loving thoughts of you.

Our love is as strong as the rarest of precious metals.
When our bud open wide our love will survive all falling petals.

Finishing Touch

Your love is like a masterpiece of fine art.
At first glance I loved you right from the start.

You came to me like a thief in the night to capture my heart.
now I'm forever yours my love until death us do part.

All the special little things you do add spice to our life.
I can feel our chemistry erupt when I take you in my arms at night.

You're my breath of fresh air at the break of each day.
You're my guiding light when the sun goes away.

I carry your scent with me as a reminder that my love awaits.
The hours we spend apart gives my heart a little ache.

Thank you for accepting me, you could have remained free.
I am truly blessed you decided to share your life with me.

Today I am rededicating my heart and soul to you.
Nothing can ever separate us, to you I'll always be true.

Your tender loving thoughts of me truly mean so much,
While embraced by your love gives it the finishing touch.

First Love

I was so young experiencing feelings I've never known before.
My heart started beating like crazy the moment he walked through the door.

I just started to develop breasts, I was embarrassed by them standing erect.
He looked at me, I felt like a queen on a chessboard, the king had me in check.

I tried to leave the room quickly, as I passed he reached out taking my arm,
I thought I was going to faint, I was completely mesmerized by his charm.

I was this awkward looking kid whose fate was left entirely to chance.
I could not believe this handsome, athletic looking guy just ask me to dance.

The music was a love song, lights were low, I was afraid of making a mistake.
I followed his lead, he held me real close to him and invited me to his place.

I was mature for my age, that I kept a secret, along with me being a virgin.
If he knew I was really young and inexperienced I would lose him as a friend.

I told him I would like to get to know him better before we started dating.
Months passed by, he started to wonder how long I would keep him waiting.

He promised to love me always, I was his woman and he was here to stay.
I knew this was the night that we were going to go all the way.

I admitted to being a virgin, continuing to lie about it didn't make any sense.
He said he knew it all along, I was unsuccessful in hiding my innocence.

Our first encounter was gentle, passionate, sensuous and handled with care.
I was completely transformed in moments, like taking a breath of fresh air.

I had just become a woman in love, bonded for life with her man.
I did not know what was ahead, on my left ring finger he placed a gold band.

He kept his promise to me, he tried to do everything he thought was right,
One year later on Valentine's Day, he made me his wife.

Give Me Back My Heart

When we would talk you could not look me in the eyes,
the day was coming when you would no longer be by my side.

When the telephone didn't ring I knew that you wouldn't dial my line,
I was in denial but I couldn't fool this old heart of mine.

I knew I had to face the lonely nights ahead all by myself,
I just can't close the book on our love and put it on a shelf.

You just didn't love me and you could not find the nerves to say good-by,
were you trying to spare me pain or you just couldn't tell me why.

How do I go on without you its hard to put all of this behind,
by letting me down easy did you think that this was would be kind.

I've had this love for you in my heart for so very long,
you turned the other way I could not understand what went wrong.

I guess I knew all along one day you would have to choose,
I could not bring myself to the reality I would be the one who lose.

Now that you've chose another and we will have to remain apart,
all I ask is for you to find a way to give me back my heart.

Guilty
Three Strikes I'm Out

I have the right to remain silent, I don't have to reveal my feelings,
I have a right to seek counsel, I need some sexual healing.

I plead the fifth on the grounds I might incriminate myself,
I'm at the mercy of your love, can't you see I need help.

1st count: charged for loving you,
2nd count: charged for wanting you,
3rd count: charged for being true.

I swear to tell the truth, nothing but the truth, let me plead my case,
I'm competing for your affections, how can I win this race?

I love only you, I can't deny the truth, there's no turning back,
Nothing is circumstantial about my love, I've stated all the facts.

I believe all is fair in love, so I took our love to new heights,
Am I guilty for loving you throughout endless nights?

This is my first offense; I throw myself on the mercy of your love,
What is the verdict going to be? I pray to the heavens above.

First count: guilty as charged for loving you the way I do,
Second count: guilty as charged for wanting no one but you,
Third count: guilty as charged for remaining true.

I'm guilty as charged on all three counts, how could you be so cold?
I'm sentenced to life in love with you without a chance of parole.

There's no escape from this prison of love, I know what you're all about,
Guilty as charged on all three counts, three strikes I'm out.

Hickory

One day my best friend came over to my house
to tell me he was moving away.

It was a sad day for me because I didn't have the words
to make him want to stay.

He said California was becoming too much for him,
and he needed a change.

I was happy he made a decision for the better,
selfishly I wanted him to remain.

Someone once said "parting is such sweet sorrow."

I can't see anything sweet about it,
all I know is I won't see him tomorrow.

He loaded up his truck and headed for the South
where he ended up in the state of Mississippi.

He once crossed over oceans and sailed a few seas.
I never once imagined him now being so far away from me.

Thank God for telephones so we can always keep in touch.
Good friends don't come so easily. I miss him very much.

Mississippi turned out to be a good move,
he is now happy and living care-free.

Will I ever see him again now that he has a new life,
somewhere in a place called Hickory.

This poem was written about a close male friend. We were in-laws. Our children married and gave us beautiful grandchildren. There is a true love between us but our friendship is stronger. I love you Otis Jones.

I Don't Know How to Stop Loving You

After all this time I thought just for a moment we could love each other again.
Just one moment in your arms sent my old feelings into a tailspin.

I can't understand why I have no control over what runs through my mind.
I still picture us over a candlelight dinner with soft music and the best wine.

I still remember the first time we met, I looked into your eyes for the first time.
It was a moment frozen in time for me, I knew no matter what you were mine.

Why can't I let go of this never-ending dream that we will find our way back.
Our love derailed along the line, I hope we could get back on track.

I threw my feelings into the raging winds, only for them to return again.
I try everyday to break free of the hold you have on me, when will it all end.

I went on with my life; I made a vow I will live to be happy and free.
I had no way of knowing that the love I had for you would live on inside of me.

I find myself reminiscing about all the special moments that we once shared.
Those moments meant so much because I believed in my heart that you cared.

I don't know when we lost one another; I don't understand what went wrong.
The only thing I am sure of is my heart has missed your loving for so very long.

I sat in a dimly lit room one night listening to old music that made me blue.
It took me down memory lane; tears came running that was long overdue.

Why can't I break away, it must be the little things that you do.
I can do just about anything else but I don't know how to stop loving you.

I Keep Seeing You

Are you just a figment of my imagination?
Will you ever materialize to relieve my sensations?
I know you're out there for me, it's like a revelation.
Listen to my heart and feel the palpitation.

Our day is coming, patience is the clue.
Every time I close my eyes I keep seeing you.

My temperature keeps right on rising with desire.
I know down in my soul only you can control this fire.
When I get into you, I reach the point of no return.
I can hear your voice in a whisper watching my soul burn.

Taking you in my arms is long overdue.
Every time I close my eyes I keep seeing you.

Kissing me all over gently, only you have the answer.
The need for you is running through me like cancer.
Turning me inside out, you are in total control.
Our passion gets deeper as we grow old.

I can feel your touch all over me, I don't know what to do.
Every time I close my eyes I keep seeing you.

I hope the time for our real life union is near.
I want to share everything I can imagine with you my dear.
When you hold out your hands for me to come, I will have no fear.
Because every time I open my eyes I will have you here.

My vision of you is as gentle as the morning dew.
Every time I close my eyes I keep seeing you.

I Knew I Could Love Again

The first time I heard your voice so warm and tender
I was addicted at once, a voice I'll always remember.

I am a strong believer true love is so hard to find,
you challenged my heart, now it's no longer mine.

How do I let you know it's only you my eyes can see,
I've been in total control until now, always running free.

I can feel you running through me, deep into my soul,
I don't know when I surrendered only that you've got a strong hold.

You took the fear out of commitment making me want to settle down,
love me unconditional and turn my whole world around.

My heart is at full throttle, racing at top speed.
I hope I'm the one you want, I know I am the one you need.

If you can't return these feelings tell me so I can step on the brake,
don't take my heart on a joy ride, my whole life is at stake.

I don't know where all these feelings are coming from or how they all begin,
the moment our eyes met for the first time I knew I could love again.

I'm Hanging Up My Hat

Sitting here at the bar having one more for the road.
Heading home for some loving these nights are getting cold.

This cowboy is ready to wash off the stale road dust.
Your love drives me; I'll reach California by sunrise or bust.

I realize being with you forever is where it's at.
No more shooting the bull with the boys, I'm cleaning up my act.
No more drifting here and there, I'm hanging up my hat.

You have been patient with me and my quest.
Get ready for your man who loves you the best.

Not holding you in my arms at night is what this cowboy will miss.
I'll travel a million miles just for the warmth of your tender kiss.

I realize being with you forever is where it's at.
I can't wait to lay with you and have our late night chats.
Trust your heart like I trust mine because I'm hanging up my hat.

No more broken promises leaving you at home alone with our cat.
Our love will be legendary just like Miss Kitty and Marshall Matt.

You hung in there with me no matter what you were told.
I'm bringing home with me my vows, my heart and a ring of gold.

I realize being with you forever is where it's at.
I won't lose you to another man cause he ain't all that.
I'm staking my claim on your love baby; I'm hanging up my hat.

Incarcerated Love

Help me understand his mind, it's so hard for me to see,
why do he keep doing foolish things if he truly does love me.

Why did he do what he did so they can take him away?
Once again I am all alone on all the family holidays.

I can hardly wait to see and talk to him on visitor's day.
can I turn my back on him, there's just no way.

I know what he did is absolutely wrong
I'll continue to wait for him it doesn't matter how long.

Every one tell me to go on with my life he's just a bad boy,
if he's so bad why does he give my heart so much joy.

Every time I think about him it always bring me to tears
what can I do to ease my forever-lingering fears.

He promised me the world, the stars, Venus and Mars,
nothing but broken promises, he's always behind bars.

He said our love will survive the test of time, he'll always be mine,
a glass wall stands between us, I have to always leave him behind.

I will always cherish the love for me he has shown,
what frightens me more than his love is the future unknown.

I pray for guidance I draw my strength from the heavens above,
then why am I so bewildered by the hold of my incarcerated love?

I Only Had One Night

The moment I looked in your eyes I knew that night was meant to be.
I was sure this was not wishful thinking by the way you looked back at me.

I could feel the chemistry between us; my pulse had a crazy beat.
The music was soft, the room dimly lit, I could hardly wait for our lips to meet.

The song that was playing at the time had become our special song.
Everything was perfect about that night nothing went wrong.

We held each other closely, introducing ourselves during our first dance.
You ask me to go home with you later, so I decided to take a chance.

We were walking under a moon lit sky when we surrendered our first kiss.
I told myself no matter what happen, this is one night I refuse to miss.

The night became more passionate as we began to explore.
I could feel the heat radiating from each other as our clothes fell to the floor.

When you took me home you ask me for my number to give me a call.
A lot of time has passed since that night, I haven't heard from you at all.

After our lovemaking was over you held me in your arms real tight.
There was nothing there to warn me I only had one night.

If Only I Told You I Care

I waited until you were no longer there.

I waited until I lost contact and couldn't find you anywhere.

I didn't express myself and let you walk away.

I was afraid to tell you I wanted you to stay.

I let my pride get in the way.

I put off for tomorrow what I should have done today.

There was no reason for us to ever say good-by.

It didn't pay for me to hold everything inside.

My feelings were there but never shown.

I took you for granted; I never thought I would end up alone.

Now I sit in the window and stare.

Wondering if things would be different if only I told you I care.

Love Don't Make Sense

We come from two different worlds with no common ground,
I can't understand the attraction, why do I even want you around.

You are so carefree with life, never making anyone a commitment,
each time we are together our love is so intense.

I don't know where this relationship is going, my mind is in a strain,
my heart is beating in slow motion, wondering if it can stand the pain.

I really don't know where all my common sense went,
the only thing I do know is love don't make sense.

My family and friends think that I am losing my mind,
they don't see you as I do, warm, gentle, passionate and kind.

Will you hang in there with me or will you walk away leaving me behind,
sometimes your actions confuse me, is love really that blind.

Be up front with me, do I see something that is not really there,
I need to know now if you're just enjoying life or if you really do care.

I really don't know where all my common sense went,
the only thing I do know is love don't make sense.

You come and go as you please, never wanting to be questioned,
is there something you are keeping from me, it this a warning.

Whenever you want to have your way, you know all the buttons to push,
I try not to give in so easily, something tells me to take a closer look.

I've tried to walk away from you, but you've got me on your hook,
you know when my head is spinning, you read me like a book.

I really don't know where all my common sense went,
the only thing I do know is love don't make sense.

Looking For My Love

I'm looking for love so my heart won't break
I'm looking for love and I can't see your face.

    I'm looking, I'm looking
    I'm looking for my love.

I've travel the highways far and wide
And I still don't have you here by my side.

    I'm looking, I'm looking
    I'm looking for my love.

I need your loving where can you be?
I need to have you here with me.

    I'm looking, I'm looking
    I'm looking for my love.

When I close my eyes at night
I'm loving you baby with all my might.

    I'm looking, I'm looking
    I'm looking for my love.

My spirit is high and my heart is free
It's all here waiting why can't you see?

    I'm looking, I'm looking
    I'm looking for my love.

I want to hold you under a moonlit sky
I can't find you baby and I don't know why?

    I'm looking, I'm looking
    I'm looking for my love.

I'm looking for love so my heart won't break
I'm looking for love and I can't see your face.

    I'm looking, I'm looking
    I'm looking for my love.

Loving You Hurts

I love you but loving you is wrong.
I love you but my patience won't last to long.

I love you but you take me for granite.
I love you but you can't seem to get it.

I love you but it's a one-way street.
I love you but your standards I cannot meet.

I love you but to you it's just a game.
I love you but I can't stand anymore pain.

I love you but there is something missing.
I love you but there is no emotion when we're kissing.

I love you but you let others get in our way.
I love you but you make it hard for me to stay.

I love you but with my heart you choose to flirt.
I love you but loving you hurts.

Loving Online

I've made burning love to your inquisitive mind.
The image of loving you never leaves my thoughts.
You have managed to penetrate my well-guarded heart.
I don't know if loving you this way is smart.

I think of you passionately with each passing moment.
I must stay in control and make sure my time is well spent.
I find myself longing to hear those words "you've got mail".
I am incarcerated electronically by your magic spell.

Although we are miles apart we are connected through chips.
How I long for your smile and to touch your tender lips.
Our passions ran away and sprouted like roses in full bloom.
Did I lose myself to you forever in our private chat room?

You have taken me to new heights where I have never been.
I tell myself I won't go back but I end up there again and again.
Will I find a way out of this crazy maze that I have stumbled in?
I miss you so much when a lot of time escapes us my special friend.

You know what I long to hear and all the right words to say.
I can't refrain myself; eventually I give in and you have your way.
Every morning I wake up to the memories of our yesterdays.
I won't know how to turn around if you ever went away.

Can real love truly evolve during our special intimate chats?
Will I surrender totally to the sound of your seductive voice, perhaps?
We have other commitments that consume the majority of our time.
Somehow we always manage to steal a moment or two for loving online.

My Marriage Vows

To the one I love,

Today is the day I open up every part of me and surrender it all to you,
our lives have just become one, you are now a part of everything I do.

Today we are reborn in our love for each other, this bond is forever,
only death can separate us, until then, we will always be together.

Before today we led separate lives, neither one of us was perfect,
those lives no longer exist, everything before today I am willing to forget.

When we join hands today it will be the first seal of our love, a new beginning,
we have just written chapter one of our life, a love story never ending.

I love everything about you, there is nothing about you I want to change,
I fell in love with this incredible person and here is where I want to remain.

I promise to love you, honor you, respect, and protect you until my last breath,
this challenge is the second seal of our love, putting our love to the test.

We will make our own decisions, keeping others out even if they mean well,
we'll make mistakes at times I'm sure, we'll recover, only time will tell.

When or if problems arise we will always work them out, never ending in a fight,
I promise we will resolve all our problems, before I close my eyes that night.

I know the first year will be challenging getting to know one another,
this is the third seal of our love, surviving the first year respecting each other.

Our learning tree will have many branches, each branch a chapter in our book,
our life will blossom to its fullest, the trunk of our tree has strong roots.

I truly accept you unconditionally, with a love that will never fall,
I promise to cherish your love forever my darling, today I am giving you my all.

No Strings Attached

You are my best friend, I trust you with my life,
I know what's in your heart, you want everything to be right.

You try hard to be this rock that has a shield from all pain,
I know when you're hurting, your eyes can't hide the strain.

I know what it's like to have loved someone in vain,
we don't always learn from mistakes sometimes we try again.

There will be times when you'll find life really hard to digest
just keep your chin up and give the world your very best.

I get excited everytime I hear the telephone ring,
there is something about you that makes my heart sing.

Next time you feel the need to love someone look my way,
I will never take your love for granted I am here to stay.

Your heart is the only thing in this world I ever wanted to steal,
maybe one day your eyes will open and you'll see that I'm for real.

When your mind strays to other pastures just remember I got your back,
my love is unconditional with no boundaries and no strings attached.

Outbreak of Memories

As I sit here in my solitude I think about our undying love,
I wonder if you're thinking about me and the way things was.

I find myself pacing back and forth across the living room,
then I walk out into the night only to see a lover's moon.

I want to say so much, I wish you could hear my thoughts,
I can hear your laughter in my mind while sitting alone in the park.

When you're away from me I feel so empty inside,
I realize how precious you are to me when my eyes open wide.

I am forever yours my darling, I've made up my mind,
our love will grow over the coming years until the end of time.

The little time we're apart its only you I truly miss,
take my hand in yours and let's seal this love with a kiss.

I thought I was immune from love but you've got the power,
my thoughts are only of loving you hour after hour.

Whenever temptation put its chokehold on me,
I think about our loving and have an outbreak of memories.

Shake Me Down

You say you love me and I am your only man,
when I come home at night you're always wearing a frown,
before I climb into bed all you want to do is shake me down.

What is it with you, why do you keep on acting like a clown?
Sometimes you act like you don't even want me around.
Everytime I turn around you're trying to shake me down.

What are you looking for searching through all my things?
I can't understand why you run to the phone everytime it ring.
I wonder what in the world tomorrow is going to bring.

I get the feeling you're following me when I go downtown.
Your jealousy is turning your foolish head around.
Whenever I'm out of sight you wanna shake me down.

Hey baby its time for you to lighten up.
How much longer do you think I'm going to put up with this stuff?
Trying to live here with you is getting pretty rough.

Your so-called friends come around giving you bad advice.
Why can't you see they would love to see us end up in a fight?
Let them tell it nothing that I am doing for you is right.

One of these days you will see they really want to be in your shoes.
They get a kick out of you running around acting like a fool.
You should have learned all this madness when you were in school.

I gave you everything you wanted, it was never enough.
I'm trying to keep our home together, but you are making it tough.
I wake up in the morning ready to give it all up.

I don't understand why you can't see you're running me in the ground.
What is it girl are you part hound?
Everytime I turn around you're trying to shake me down.

Today We Wed

Today with love I take thee Gregory.
Today with love I take thee Celeste.
We are bound together in total commitment,
our love has survived all the tests.

We love each other unconditionally,
and will love each other more tomorrow.
We will rejoice in our love now and forever,
today we celebrate our love without any sorrow.

We'll cross the threshold of our new life,
only to open up brand new doors, its time to begin.
Our families are now joined together by our love,
with the strength of family behind us we can only win.

We both could have taken different paths,
but we have chosen to love each other instead.
We'll hold this day sacred for rest of our life,
On this special day Gregory and Celeste will wed.

When All Time Stopped

I watched you running towards me through the meadow plains.
Is this a mirage toying with my mind? Am I no longer sane.

I lost you to another with no chance of reconcile this very year.
Why are you heading my way? Is it to taunt me my dear.

As you draw near I see sunlight dancing through your hair.
When you lose your heart needlessly the game of love is no longer fair.

My mind says to turn and run before you reach your intended mark.
My soul was in danger of your spell right from the very start.

Now that we've parted you continue to add to my confusion.
Is there a love antidote or a simple love transfusion.

Woe is me to have stumbled and fallen so deep,
into this web of love you spun and no doubt intend to keep.

Don't come any closer unless you are totally devoted to me.
End my needless suffering, my heart is in peril can't you see.

Don't wet my lips with just enough passion to make me linger,
release me from this bond you have before I die and wither.

Are my ears deceiving me? You realized you made a mistake.
Our love will survive these tests of time, togetherness is our fate.

Remember the night we spent together on that magical mountaintop,
a special moment in our love when all time stopped.

When You Realized You Needed Me

The first night we met, we were both happy and free,
we talked for hours about our lives and how our future could be,
our first date was a night to remember throughout the years,
That was when you realized you needed me.

We were all wrapped up in each other, as happy as can be,
no one could come between us, it wasn't hard for anyone to see,
we were destined for each other, we had beat all the odds,
That was when you realized you needed me.

When we made love it was complete ecstasy,
new feelings were released we didn't know we had,
we were meant for each other, this we both believed,
That was when you realized you needed me.

Years have gone by gracefully, so have our maturity,
your appetite for life kept changing, so let it be,
the day came when you felt you had to be free,
That was when you felt you no longer needed me.

Your happiness was all that ever really mattered to me.
I am willing to let you go if it's what you really need.
Whatever you're looking for I truly hope you find.
I have to start all over again and put the past behind.

Now that my freedom was handed back so willingly,
I have a lot of things to work out, now I see things differently,
I'm a new person now and have a new way of thinking,
I've come to realize that all I need is to believe in me.

I'm sorry the dream you went after didn't turn out right,
I hate to see you hurting when you go home at nights,
there's no chance for us after all this time, I'm sure you see,
especially now that you realized all you ever needed was me.

When The Past Comes Back

There was a voice on the line from my past asking do you remember me?
A voice that triggered a lot of bad memories I thought had set me free.

I am confused, I realized popularity is not such a good thing,
you never know what being popular is going to bring.

All the things I've forgotten or chose not to remember,
sent chills through my body like a cold night in December.

The time has come when I have to put all my cards on the table,
I look into my children eyes and wonder if I am truly able.

I have to tell them there was a time when I was not so refine,
a time in my life when I experimented with drugs, marijuana and wine.

No excuses for my actions it was mostly out of a need to escape from reality,
it didn't take long for me to realize this was not my personality.

Will my children be upset with me behind my indiscretions?
or will they forgive me and accept that I've learned tough lessons.

This is why I discipline them when they are headed in the wrong direction,
I've been there, done that and I was trying to share my acquired wisdom.

Will my past change the way they see me or affect their lives forever,
if I knew my past would hurt my children would I repeat my sins, never, never?

Every decision made I had my children best interest at heart,
I had to keep us together, no matter what I was not going to have us torn apart.

I will never bow my head in shame, I will again fall under somebody's attack,
I pray for unconditional love from my children when the past comes back.

Why Did You Take My Love If You Didn't Know What To Do With It?

I gave you everything I had, when all I had to give was me,
before you showed your selfish ways I was happy and free.

You let me believe I was your special one and you really care,
you wanted me all to yourself and refuse to share.

I took the four walls we share turned it into a home,
a place you can call your own so you won't have to roam.

I took the food we brought home turned it into a meal,
given a slight chance at me your friends will try to steal.

I took the seed you planted inside me carried it to full term,
I gave you a beautiful child a love you didn't have to earn.

You had to know in your heart what you were doing was not right,
who in the hell gave you the right to toy with my life?

You led me to believe that our love was on solid ground,
why did you hang around if you knew you were going to let me down?

I don't know what makes your mind lose focus and run astray,
what's the matter you can't make up your mind to go or stay?

You had your chance, took advantage of me, now I won't take this shit,
why did you take my love if you didn't know what to do with it?

Wind Carry My Love Home

Wind I always lose myself in your pleasant embrace.
You tranquilize my soul comforting my heartache.

You seem to know when I need to have you here.
When the peril of life overwhelm me you ease my fears.

Times when I am feeling abandoned you are there for me.
I truly understand now that the best things in life are free.

You lift my spirits reminding me I am not totally alone.
After a walk with you it brings tranquillity to my home.

Wind please harvest my emotions and carry them with you.
In your travels maybe you'll meet someone who feel the way I do.

If there is someone out there who share my feelings let them see.
There is a true love waiting and bring them home to me.

Wind you know all the qualities I want in my mate.
I put all my trust in your scrutiny so I will continue to wait.

Tell my love to trust his heart and head my way.
I am excited with anticipation of our first day.

Wind whisper words of devotion while you roam.
I depend on you so please Wind carry my love home.

You Couldn't See for Looking

Honey, we use to party all night and have a good time.
Every weekend all you wanted to do was wine and dine.

You called ahead to tell me to get ready and put on my flashy red dress.
Don't worry about anything else you would take care of all the rest.

When the DJ started playing music you would dance with me all night.
Over a candlelight dinner you ask me to become your wife.

After the kids came consuming all my time and me picking up a little weight.
You started going out without me partying and you didn't even hesitate.

Years of emotional neglect; I shed the excess pounds and put on a new dress.
I'm back on the dance floor partying with old friends and looking my best.

Now you're talking about staying home and showing you a little respect.
You should have thought about that years ago now I have to put you in check.

You waited to long and let me out of my unattended little cage.
If you need me for anything now sugar you're going to have to page.

Now you're jumping into your car following me all around.
Another man came into your territory and walked on sacred ground.

I know you want us to start all over again.
I'm sorry it won't happen baby I'm enjoying my new friend.

You want me to come home you miss my loving and my good cooking.
You were blind to the good thing you had, you couldn't see for looking.

FANTASY

A Face in the Crowd

People see the entertainer as living a glorious life,
with all the parties, gilt, glamour and their name in bright lights.

No one knows when I'm out on that stage performing with all my might,
I'm looking for that one face in the crowd, I can go home to at night.

My fans are my motivating force with a packed house as far as I can see,
I'm still looking for that one face in the crowd, who can truly see me.

I try to isolate myself from fame hunters, it's hard to tell who they are,
I'm looking for that face in the crowd whose looking at me, not at a star.

Pretenders with habits will consume you, possibly give you a stroke,
when everything you worked hard for could all end up in smoke.

When I meet someone new I wonder will they always stand by my side,
do they really care, or if they are just going along for the ride.

I can't afford to take the chance of losing my heart again on a whim,
true love is suppose to come free, my chances look kind of slim.

It is so confusing being in a crowd of people and feeling so alone,
will a face ever appear in the crowd who will be waiting for me at home.

My friends try to set me up with dates, I frown when I get their page,
I sing about that special someone when I step out on the stage.

I see a lot of faces in the audience, my devoted fans are here to stay,
I still don't see the one face in the crowd that will never go away.

My song to my lover would say my love has no boundaries,
my love will be a true love, you won't have to worry about a rivalry.

I've sang my last song, the concert is over, I've taken my final bow,
My heart is beating wildly, I believe I see a face in the crowd.

Day Dreams

I love daydreaming.
I can go anywhere, do anything, be anyone I want to be.
I can have anything I want, and anyone I want that appeals to me.

I can be a pilot soaring 50,000 feet into the sky,
I can be a submarine captain diving to the depths of the ocean to hide.

I can be a princess standing on a balcony being serenaded by my prince.
I can be Jane swinging from tree to tree with Tarzan and our little chimps.

I can be the first lady standing along side our president.
I can be Cleopatra with Mark Anthony sailing in the long ships.

I can join the Star Trek crew on the Enterprise to explore the stars.
I can travel with Aladdin on a magic carpet ride no matter how far.

I can be a beautiful ballerina on stage dancing my best,
I can turn into something bad like the wicked witch of the West.

I can turn into Ginger Rogers and dance all night with Fred Astaire.
I can hop in a convertible car with James Dean and become the wild pair.

I can travel to Hong Kong and become the elusive Susie Wong.
I can end up in uncharted jungle captured by an ape called King Kong.

In this computer age of illusion and virtual reality it seems,
nothing is more exhilarating than my daydreams.

Forbidden Lover

Forbidden Lover of mine how long do we continue to meet on the shy?
After a sensuous night of lovemaking we always have to say good-by.

Your vows were made to another woman when you took her hand.
I can't help the way I feel I'm hopelessly in love with a married man.

At the end of everyday I wonder will you get the chance to slip away.
We both know one of these days we're going to have to pay.

Forbidden Lover of mine you have the best of both worlds,
a wife who vowed for better or worse and me who can never come first.

Every night I dream about us and everything is always just right.
We spend so little time with each other there is never a reason to fight.

Forbidden Lover of mine all I want to do is love you with all my heart.
Your family obligations are the only thing keeping us apart.

Why do I keep letting my feelings get in the way? I know this is wrong.
There is no future in loving a married man I can't keep holding on.

When the holiday seasons roll around I have to spend them all alone.
You spend all the holidays with your wife and children at home.

Sometimes when I'm alone listening to music that remind me of you,
I come to the realization that I will always be number two.

Forbidden Lover of mine I try to resist you but you control my fate.
We both know how easily love can turn into hate.

Forbidden Lover the day will come when you are going to have to choose.
I'm the outside woman in love I will be the one who loses.

I need to have you in my life lover even if it's for a very short time.
I will love you until the end of our time forbidden lover of mine.

Intimate Moments In My Mind

A place where I can go where no one can ever spy,
a place where I can love freely underneath a clear blue sky.

A place where my feelings are not on a roller coaster ride,
where love is in the air and there is no reason to run and hide.

A place with no rules or expectations I am completely free,
where I am in control and everything feels good to me.

A place where feelings run deep, there is no right or wrong,
where I can drift into complete ecstasy all the day long.

A place where hearts join together and never part,
where love is strong and true right from the very start.

A place where spontaneous loving is totally unplanned,
where time has no set boundaries love as long as you can.

A place where little things from the heart mean so much,
where nothing is more precious than the gentleness of a touch.

I know what I am doing is nothing put pure unadulterated lust,
for my own sanity it's escape into fantasy land or bust.

Escape from the pains of reality is really hard to find,
nothing is more extraordinary than intimate moments in my mind.

I Want An Old Fashion Man

I want a man who will make me the center of his world.
Showering me with love and devotion not just diamonds and pearls.

I want a man when he looks at me it feels like a natural high.
I want him to lose himself completely when he looks into my eyes.

I want him to hold my hand when we walk down the street.
I want him to be proud when he introduces me to people we meet.

Before he gets into the car he will first open my door.
I want him to hold me tight as we tango on the dance floor.

I want the romantic meals eaten by candlelight.
I want the passionate kisses in the heat of the night.

I want to enter his mind every time his heart beats.
I want him honest and faithful; one who will never cheat.

My man has to be my companion, my lover and my friend.
He has to have an undying love for me until the end.

Our love life will be devoted totally to monogamy.
I don't want to share his love with anyone other than me.

I want to feel secure and safe when he holds me in his arms.
I want to laugh at the silly things he does when he turns on his charm.

I want my man to respect and support me in the things I want to do.
When the going gets tough I know he's there for me to turn to.

I will love and honor him faithfully like nobody else can.
I will hold on to this dream because I want an old fashion man.

Much Right Man

He is a much right man who is still free,
until he take his vows there is still a chance for me.

He is a much right man whom I have an obsession,
before it's all over he will be solely in my possession.

He is a much right man, once he's had a taste of me,
you might as well back down girl, I'm all he'll be able to see.

He is a much right man, I want more than a casual fling,
when I get him in my arms to me he'll forever cling.

He is a much right man every time he comes around,
I lose control of my senses while my heart just pounds and pounds.

He is a much right man whose sweat drips off him like honey,
he's got everything I'll ever need it's not all about money.

He is a much right man any woman would be proud,
he has my head dancing high in a cloud.

He is a much right man who still has a right to choose,
as long as he's single I have just as much right as you do.

I'll hang in there forever and ever or as long as I can,
as long as his heart and mind are free he's a much right man.

My Enchanting Sea

Sea my enchanting sea.
You've always been a complete mystery to me.

I love a moonlit night when the sea is dead calm.
It looks like a highway to eternity no one can see beyond.

It really mystifies me when the sea goes out with the tide.
It seems as though its inhabitants are trying to run and hide.

I marvel in the waves pounding against high mountain cliffs.
I get excited watching the seamen set sails on their long ships.

Sea my beautiful sea your horizons are never ending.
No matter what end I start from it all looks like a beginning.

It's a miracle in itself how you sustain a multitude of life.
All the colorful sea creatures swimming around with all their might.

I love to hear the seagulls flying above you trying to converse.
Birds are so extraordinary because nothing they do is rehearsed.

I love to listen to the seamen's tall sea tales.
I also love to see the mating of those beautiful whales.

One thing for sure man will never be able to conquer you.
When seamen return home safe it's because you let them pass through.

When my time here has expired and I must pass on.
I want my ashes taken out to sea because we have a special bond.

Sea my beautiful sea please don't ever forget me.
I want to leave a part of me behind in a place I cherish; my enchanting sea.

My Valentine

You are the guiding light in my life,
I'm engulfed in your love from morning till night.

Your smile is bright as the afternoon sunlight,
you have my heart on a string flying it like a kite.

I am eagerly awaiting your soft gentle kiss,
when we're apart it's your kisses I truly miss.

Your scent is like a bouquet of spring flowers,
a scent that lingers in my mind hour after hour.

Thinking of you throws my heart off its track,
my heart runs away and then bounces right back.

On this special day for lovers let's cherish it always,
our love lights will shine bright forever and a day.

Right now our love is in full bloom,
you came into my life not a moment too soon.

The key to my heart only you hold,
the symbol of our love is a single red rose.

Please accept this old lovesick heart of mine,
caress my undying love and be My Valentine.

Parakeet Sing For Me

You have all the colors of life spread throughout your wings,
so beautiful and serene what do all your colors mean.

You always soar so gracefully through the air,
sitting on a limb with your mate you're such a beautiful pair.

Is it really selfish of me to put you in a cage,
do you understand I adore you this is not an act of rage.

I never want us to separate or have to live apart,
when you soared through the air you landed on my heart.

I knew right from the first moment we met,
I want to care for you always as my darling little pet.

I know your nature is to fly freely and forever roam,
your exquisite singing brightens up my empty home.

I want to love, care, protect and treat you so kind,
accept my love little birdie of mine.

Do I keep you forever or let you go free,
Parakeet Parakeet sing for me.

Poet's Dream

As a child growing up I was infatuated with nursery rhymes,
long ones, short ones, funny ones, sad ones, there were all kinds.

I never understood why Jack and Jill created so much laughter,
I cried when Jack fell down, broke his crown and Jill came tumbling after.

I was sad when I heard Humpty Dumpty fell and broken into all those pieces,
I would cry when I heard those rhymes and I was tired of all the kid's teases.

I love bedtime stories of little animals that live in the forest trees,
I never heard it told more beautifully than through poetry.

Words kept dancing in my head; I was not ready to release them yet.
I had a vision, I knew within my heart I wanted to be a poet.

A new poem was born to me it seems like every single day.
Each one expresses life as I saw it in my own artistic way.

It is my dream my writings will bring my audience to tears.
Imagine people all over the world reading my words year after year.

The day I started writing my feelings I ask myself what does this all mean.
It suddenly dawn on me this was a reality it was no longer a poet's dream.

Songwriter

I'm a songwriter, I express myself through my lyrics,
always looking for that special song, hoping to say this is it.

Inspirations come without warning, so I have to stop and write it down,
words jump in and out of my mind, they don't just hang around.

I think about that special someone and the feelings just start flowing,
I give into my heart and mind to see which way its going.

I always go full force with what I truly know,
my words make a statement about me, it's not just a talent show.

As a songwriter I've developed my own style, that's hard to duplicate,
it's a tribute to a writer when other writers try to imitate.

I write according to my many different moods,
hoping one of my best songs a famous singer could use.

There are two or three special stars I want to sing my songs,
I choose my lyrics carefully, trying not to take to long.

Once my words are put to music and a famous singer sings them out loud,
the ultimate high is when my own words make me proud.

When people begin to recognize my talent and hire me for what I know,
I have to stay completely focused and not develop an ego.

I want my songs to be enjoyed by both the young and old,
if they listen to the words carefully, they will hear a story being told.

I want to leave something of me behind that's not just a mystery,
it would be my life's reward to hear my songs become a part of history.

Stage Fright

I am a brand new Artist finally living a dream come true.
Every time I look out at the stage my face turns a deep blue.

I start thinking about all the people who will be looking up at me.
I can't stop my knees from shaking; I know everyone will see.

How in the world will I ever get pass this crazy fear.
The sweat pouring down my face will also hide my tears.

What if I get out on that stage and cannot keep my cool.
I am so afraid of making a mistake and end up looking like a fool.

I don't feel like I am about to make a fantastic start.
I have to keep my head on straight; I can't let myself fall apart.

I hope the audience out there will fall in love with my talent.
If they do the all the time that I put into this project was well spent.

My heart is beating fast and my stomach is full of butterflies.
If I am unable to pull this off I know I will run and hide.

Family and friends are encouraging me to perform; they are by my side.
They feel my career will take off and I will travel worldwide.

Everyday when I get home I practice into the wee hours of the night.
I go over my material again and again so my memory will be airtight.

I will do my best to ignore my fears and make sure everything comes out right.
If I live through my first performance I will be able to handle my stage fright.

The Artist

Artists will sit down in front of a white canvas that's bare,
they dig deep inside themselves for inspiration to put something there.

Their brushes move gracefully like magic wands,
bristles stroking the canvas using their mystical charm.

Mixing and matching colors they use great care,
spreading the colors gently and evenly everywhere.

When their vision begin to materialize,
the artists start adding touches of elegance in strides.

They isolate themselves from everyone,
and stay in self-confinement until the paintings are done.

It may take months or sometime years,
when you see the artist's soul on canvas, it can bring you to tears.

The true reward after the long, mind boggling haul,
is to see the artist's work hanging on a famous gallery's wall.

People come to the gallery, some stand while others sit in chairs,
with admiration for the artists, they would sit for hours and stare.

When people look at the paintings they see a great story told,
the paintings get more valuable as it grows old.

The true beauty of the artist's eternal creation,
it will continue to pass down from generation to generation.

The Wind

Where do you come from?
Where do you go?
Do you just circle around the world?
I would really like to know.

Some days you are so mild,
Some days you are extremely strong,
Some days you come with a vengeance,
Did we as a people do something wrong?

Some days you come as a gentle breeze,
Some days you carry around pollen making me sneeze,
Some days you move the clouds like bouncing balls
Some days you won't show yourself at all.

Then there are times when you whirl in as a hurricane,
Causing us to board up our homes and not use our airplanes,
Other times you come as a cyclone,
These are times we wish you would leave us alone.

On one hand you have my admiration,
On the other hand you are a frustration,
Often you give us quite a scare.
Then there are times we love the wind in our hair.

You're like the many faces of Eve
Always got something up you sleeve
Never knowing what to expect
You can be kind or leave our lives in a wreck.

Wind if you really do care
I believe you won't give us more than we can bear,
we are so use to having you there,
We can live without you because you're our air.

I welcome the gentle air that you always lend,
I'm forever in your debt because you are the Wind.

Tick Tock

Do you ever feel that you've lived this day before,
you know what's going to happen before your feet hit the floor.

Your stomach is bunched up with hundreds of butterflies,
you wonder if you've lived before or is it time to say good-by.

You wake up in the morning with more hair on your chin,
you want the day to hurry up and come to an end.

Hurry, hurry, hurry everyone in always in a mad rush,
work, work, work, before you know it you're out of touch.

It feels like your life is going by extremely fast,
what is suppose to be your future is now your past.

Life is taking its toll and you wonder what's next,
you pray for peace of mind before your last dying breath.

I watch that old second hand move around that old clock,
with every beat of my heart go tick tock, tick tock, tick tock.

Wind Chimes

Wind chimes softly playing through gentle breezes.
Always playing a different tune, each one new releases.

Tiny little replicas of various life forms cast in shining metal.
Each one has a story behind it they all want to tell.

Listen to the wind chimes hear what they have to say.
Open your mind to their songs before the wind goes away.

Wind chimes softly playing in the corner of my mind.
What are you saying today; for you I'll always have time.

When the wind dies down you won't make a sound.
You just hang there waiting for the wind to come around.

Wind chimes we have something in common too.
I love the wind just as much as you do.

Wind chimes you and the wind are having a beautiful affair.
I have those same intimate moments when the wind blows through my hair.

When I brought you home and heard your music for the first time.
I knew the three of us belong together, me, the wind, and my wind chimes.

Without Dreams

Without dreams there are no roads to travel.

No hope

No goals

No beginning

No ending

No challenge

No success

No failure

No imagination

No fulfillment

No disappointment

No control

No sacrifice

It all starts with a dream as hopeless as it may seem,
it takes all you've got, there is no in between.

Every challenge we face makes up our self-esteem,
we can never be true achievers without dreams.

CELEBRITY

Cuong Phu Tran

I watched this elderly man pass by my window walking twice a day.
He could barely make it but he found strength to endure anyway.

I admired him for his diligence in continuing his daily exercise,
I could tell just by watching this elderly man somehow I knew he was wise.

Although his steps were very small, he held on to his cane; never did he fall.
I began to wonder about his youth, I suspect he use to stand pretty tall.

A distinguished looking man he is; always dressed very well.
I knew this senior man had a lot of interesting stories to tell.

Today I introduced myself to him in the front yard and we began to talk.
I told him how much I wanted to know him so I joined him in his walk.

He told me about his experiences as a soldier in the Vietnamese military.
I could tell even after all the years passed those memories still made him weary.

He was thrown in a prison camp for collaborating with the US Government.
Put there for reeducation; tortured each day during the ten years he spent.

Helping soldiers escape tortures awaiting them was said to have been wrong.
He sacrificed a lot to help our soldiers escape now he can never return home.

Righteous people will go to any length to help others, they don't care how far.
Even living in America with a new identity never revealing who you really are.

I truly hope you can return home some day to be with your family again.
God bless you for helping bring our boys home from Vietnam Cuong Phu Tran.

Maya Angelou

You have become a household name.
Your magnificent artistry is your claim to fame.

You are definitely a phenomenal woman.
If anyone can strut their stuff gracefully you can.

You're like an exotic flower that's a rare breed.
Blooming in the sunshine of love spreading your seeds.

Your words are carried lovingly over endless seas.
When spoken softly they are like a gentle breeze.

Your style of writing gives new meaning to words.
They are the most powerful expressions I've ever heard.

Your writings tell us you've seen a lot of things in your life.
Nothing came easy; you didn't turn and run instead you chose to fight.

Your poems celebrating women was written with a lot of pride.
Your message tell women to stand tall they have nothing to hide.

You've sparked the hopes of every poet to become as great as you.
That is why this poem was written, a tribute long overdue.
A new star is shining bright in the galaxy and its called Maya Angelou.

I love this woman. I remember saving my money so that I could go to hear her speak at Hayward State University in California. Maya was so eloquent in her manner of delivery. I enjoyed every minute of her recital. I gave her this poem in a blue frame with a ribbon attached to it. I do hope she enjoyed it. I never had a chance to speak with her. She is truly a "Phenomenal Woman".

OPRAH WINFREY

Oprah, a name so unique what does it truly mean?
You've penetrated the hearts of millions so it seems.

People love you, trust you and consider you their personal friend,
there is no one you've met whose heart you did not win.

One thing for sure that's prevalent in your everyday actions,
your honest concern for humanity shown by your compassion.

You listen to, laugh with people and sometimes you even cry,
you share your own experiences never worrying about your pride.

You address issues some people consider a terrible sin,
you challenge injustice put it behind you and start all over again.

You embody qualities that you manage to bring out in others,
you're an inspiration to all; even young mothers.

The name Oprah has a luminous definition:

> O is for Outstanding
> P is for Prestigious
> R is for Remarkable
> A is for Achiever
> H is for Humanitarian

All these qualities bring you the highest recognition.

Being a success is only a fraction of who you are,
one thing for sure you are definitely a bright shining star.

You're leaving a courageous path behind that will be written in history,
I'm honored to witness your benevolent life Oprah Winfrey.

What can I possibly say about this woman that has not already been said? I rarely get to watch her show because of the hours I work. When I do I marvel in her inner beauty. One of my dreams is to be featured in her book club. That would be the ultimate achievement for me. Little does Oprah know she paved a road only the dedicated at heart can travel. Thank you Oprah for being one of my beacons in the night.

Ten Decades

1ST Decade	You develop, experience puberty and learn.
2nd Decade	You train real hard so good wages you can earn.
3rd Decade	You marry, work harder because you have big dreams.
4th Decade	You find out from circumstances what family truly mean.
5th Decade	You watch your children mature and finally leave home.
6th Decade	You watch your children start families of their own.
7th Decade	You watch your grandchildren grow like tumbleweeds.
8th Decade	You marvel in what started just from one of your seeds.
9th Decade	You see all your offspring in a beautiful parade.
10th Decade	Now you can sit back and rest after ten decades.

I went to Ed Williams's 100th birthday party here at LaBuona Vita Park. His sight was poor and had very little hearing left. I read the poem sitting real close to him. He said out of all the gifts he received he loved this poem the best. His life was a true love story. He passed away shortly after the party. I am glad I got a chance to know him.

Pavarotti

I never heard an earthly sound more exhilarating than thee.
Your voice is so captivating it completely paralyzes me.

You are the greatest tenor to ever walk this earth.
When you come to town in concert everyone empties their purse.

You sing with such poise, grace and flare.
Every time you walk out on a stage to perform I wish I were there.

Nessum dorma rips through my inner being when you sing that song.
It takes me to another dimension in time, I forget where I belong.

You always sing with such strong emotions and feelings.
It's like experiencing a spiritual healing.

Listening to you sing truly makes me want to fall in love.
Your fascinating voice takes flight like a graceful white dove.

The three tenors concert felt like three Angels on tour from Heaven.
Those combined tenor voices will never be forgotten.

Your voice will be remembered by all until the end of time.
Your voice is embedded in the hearts of millions favorite tenor of mine.

Luciano, Luciano your voice has completely enslaved me.
No other voice can move me the way you do my dear Pavarotti.

Pavarotti's voice is true poetry. I purchased his Three Tenors concert on video. I lose myself everytime I hear him sing. Days when I am at a low I'd play his concert. His voice reminds me of all the beauty in this world..

SPORTS

Football

Both teams are introduced as they come out on the field,
their minds racing, hearts beating fast with excitement that won't yield.

Everyone stops for a moment to acknowledge our red, white and blue,
afterward fans start roaring so loud you can feel the hype running through you.

A coin is tossed in the air, while a team member chooses heads or tails,
cheerleaders doing their thing on the sidelines, listen to their wail.

Quarterback hoping and praying that his linemen will cover his hide,
trying to get away from those outside linebackers coming from both sides.

Quarterback receives the ball, looking for an opening in the flat,
look who jumped in the air catching the ball, his faithful runningback.

Runningback carries the ball 30 yards until the safety takes him to the ground,
this game is giving me a rush, he only five yards from a touchdown.

Quarterback's last chance to win a tied game, he fights off another attacker,
scurrying around, launching the ball, dodging those linebackers.

The last two minutes of a close game will surely tell it all,
no other game makes me climb the walls in suspense as football.

It takes my breath away every time they reach the five-yard line,
the clock ran out, score is tied, the game goes into overtime.

Coin is tossed on the 50-yard line for the second time,
Offense in a huddle, making plans to run past the 1-yard line.

Runningback catches the ball almost getting tackled to the ground,
holding the ball tight praying he won't fumble, 30, 20, 10, 5 yards, touchdown.

The fans going crazy in the stands, look at them run up and down the halls,
there's nothing more exciting than this game they call football.

EMOTIONS

A Million Can Win

I am truly blessed that I lived long enough to see such a historical day.
When one million black men turned toward Washington and headed that way.

Today I witnessed proud black men pledge to make a brand new start.
A million black men of all ages joined in together and they marched.

They came in congregations, one by one and in pairs to hear their leaders talk.
United for the first time since Dr. King had his vision and they walked.

They wore their pride like a suit of armor while they sang their hymns,
there was not one violent man among all these proud black men.

The whole world watched with complete astonishment,
as these peaceful black men came forward seeking their atonement.

These black men made a pact that was clearly understood,
they will return home to make a difference in their neighborhood.

I was proud to see all the generations of black men come together,
grandfathers, fathers, uncles, sons, nephews and brothers.

They decided to join forces in this dynamic task,
pledging war on criminals and drug dealers to take their streets back.

It's good to see these men stand proud and accept their responsibilities,
educate their children, showing them why we fought to be free.

One million black men departed the next day on a brand new mission,
putting the black families back together without the majority's permission.

This is a day I will always remember; passing it down to my next of kin,
the pledge of united black men showing the world a million can win.

Affirmative Action

Equal opportunity is suppose to be the American way,
the opposition does not intend to let affirmative action stay.

Politicians say America no longer has a need for this protection,
reverse discrimination is the weapon of their objections.

Nineteen ninety-five is the year we turn back the hands of time,
this time our Capitol Hill politicians have truly crossed the line.

Politicians are using hard times to turn people against each other,
campaigning, walking through crowds, calling people brother.

Their sole purpose is to put minorities and women "back in their places",
they speak, making false statements while looking in the people faces.

America is full of good people, that's how we became a great nation,
one thing that won't happen is the chosen few won't return to plantations.

They want the people to turn on one another until Affirmative Action is gone,
this way people won't focus on the politicians and see what's really going on.

No education, no social security, no balanced budget, no equal opportunity,
our children have a lot to look forward to, America with no unity.

Politicians want the people to go out of their way every four years and vote,
knowing that when the time come the people's choices they will revoke.

Democracy is what our ancestors fought and died for so we may live in peace,
our forefathers are disgraced by our leaders who lie and continue to cheat.

The bottom line is the "Good Old Boys" find themselves losing control,
they are afraid of losing their lavish lifestyles and taking on a different role.

It's time for the American people to come out in mass numbers,
this has always been the American way if the people would only remember.

Let's travel the time line back in history and take a few more notes,
the American people will make a difference if we all come out and vote.

Stop looking for that perfect leader with no flaws, remember people are human,
start looking for the right person to lead, one who truly believes in our freedom.

Am I Sane

The pains from down deep want to rise up and shout,
I'm so hollow inside I can't turn about.

All the agony of defeat I hold within,
I lay myself upon the altar grieving in sin.

Life why do you torment my every move,
why is it me you always choose to use.

You've covered me with the tainted web you've spun,
I will hold my ground not retreat and run.

I'm ascending from the depths of a living hell,
scorched on the surface but my spirit is well.

There are days when I am left in a state of total confusion,
the marriage of love and pain is a deadly illusion.

Do I throw my feelings out into the raging winds,
only for them to come back and hurt me again.

It's getting harder to decide whose right or wrong,
I pray this mad hysteria won't last to long.

I shall not be moved by evil or fall along the wayside,
a soil gathering of minds will never abide.

My tears are camouflage by the falling rain,
My soul cries out, am I sane.

Back From Decension

I'm back from decension.
I've been living in a hollow grave.
Why didn't I pay more attention?
I gave up on myself by letting things get in the way.

I'm back from decension.
I've let my physical self run astray.
I gave into the force of depression.
I decided I'm not going out this way.

I'm back from decension.
I'm going to heal my emotional scars.
No more feelings of apprehension.
Today I decided to reach for the stars.

I'm back from decension.
I'm reclaiming what the past took from me.
My mind is in a state of positive retention.
My first breath of fresh air; I'm free.

I'm back from decension.
My chin is up and I won't hold my head down.
I've learned to live by my decisions.
The time has come for me to stand my ground.

I'm back from decension.
There's no other way for me to go but up.
I won't allow anyone in my life with bad intentions.
I've shed my facade and I'm ready to strut my stuff.

One step up at a time I can feel my transition.
I'm on the stairsteps of ascension.
I abandon negativity; I'm sending out positive transmissions.
With the help of God I made it back from decension.

Saddle Tramp

You're just a wild thing in those skin-tight jeans.
You are driving me insane do you know what I mean.

Love me or leave me no more of your childish acts.
Accept me for what I am you can't change me that's a fact.

I can't cope with your childish ways and all your crazy drama.
If you can't handle the situation go on back home to your mama.

I was up-front with you baby nothing caught you by surprise.
I am just a cattle-driving man who loves to rodeo and ride.

Now you're trying to stake your claim on me and want to marry.
Eliminate my campfire nights with the boys on the lonesome prairie.

I love you baby and hope you decide to hang around.
I want you in my life, love me for me stop putting me down.

I ain't settling down, not yet, I'm not ready to set up camp.
Love this cowboy the way I am, I'm just a saddle tramp.

I Am Who I Believe I Am

Sometime I wonder if I will succeed when people cast a doubt,
my challenge when this happens is to cast all the doubts out.

I have to be aware of the things people choose not to mention,
I have to really focus in on a person's true intentions.

I won't live my life with my mind always in a state of negative,
I'll challenge myself every day to only focus on the positive.

I will not let someone's opinion of me become my reality,
I refuse to let their assumptions disguise my true personality.

There are times when people make it real hard for me to be kind,
I have to constantly make decisions to leave all these people behind.

I side step suspicious people who are really too bold,
I won't allow them to confuse me or make me lose control.

In order for me to reach my goals I must believe in myself,
when I run into barriers I can't be too proud to ask someone for help.

I do realize there are some things I cannot accomplish all alone,
if I keep this in mind I can prevent a few things from going wrong.

I can never doubt myself no matter what, not one tiny little strand,
I will truly make it as long as I am who I believe I am.

Black Like Me

You say you understand my struggle.
How can you unless you've fought in my battles?
There's no way you can know what it is to be black.
Even if you dyed your skin for one day you can always go back.

You say you understand my pain.
How can you unless you're wearing the same stain?
If you're bewildered just look at our children's tear stained faces.
All we ask for in life is equality among the races.

You say you understand my fears.
How can you unless you've barely survived all these years?
Do you remember your mother's eyes always filled with tears?
Father pleading for humanity and no one hears.

You say you understand my fate.
How can you unless your world if full of hate?
Strong will people that we are we don't give up; we wait.
Justice with double standards always comes late.

You say you understand my hell.
How can you unless your children are in jail?
A family's hard-earned money is spent on bail.

You say all we need is an education.
If that were true we could resist temptation.
Then why are we deprived in this free nation.

You say we'll living in the land of the free.
You ask how bad could it really be?
You'll never understand unless you're black like me.

Daddy Don't

I remember looking up at your face from the cradle of your arms.
I saw the love in your eyes for me so tender and warm.

I remember the gentle kisses you gave me on the top of my head.
I remember the stories you told me when you tuck me in bed.

I remember jumping on your lap when you set down in a chair.
I remember you picking me up and tossing me up in the air.

I loved it when we would play the hide and seek game.
I hid under the bed laughing when you called out my name.

Then came the day when you loved me too much.
I never thought that I would ever be afraid of your touch.

I am confused I thought that I was still daddy's cute little girl.
The one with ponytails, ribbons and cute little curls.

Now when you ask me to come to you it makes me so sad.
I don't know what I did to make all the good things we had go bad.

You were suppose to be my hero not the one I have to fear.
What use to be love in my eyes are now only tears.

You promised me the world on a silver platter.
Now when you make promises it doesn't even matter.

When you have the desire for me and I pray that you won't.
Always remember I am flesh of thy flesh so daddy don't.

Desensitized Minds

Our youth today appear to be losing their sensitivity.
Desensitizing themselves is their coping mechanism to reality.

Influenced by peer pressure they are losing their true identity.
Desperate to belong to something they compromise their dignity.

Mindless pretense of finding humor in the face of danger.
Gangs, drugs and violence plague them, why is there so much anger?

The violence must stop before it takes another life.
They can't continue to wake up everyday preparing for another fight.

Their focus is carrying firearms to defend or make a name for themselves.
They can't see a way out of this imposed living hell.

No matter where they go desensitized minds is everywhere.
We must intervene to show them there are people who sincerely care.

Our youth need guidance, understanding and a lot of compassion.
We have to pave their way back to morality, it's time to take action.

Arm ourselves with faith when we enter their war zone.
Love, patience and forgiveness will allow us to bring our children home.

We must restore their hopes for a future that will leave all the violence behind.
Teach them to love, cherish and respect life without desensitized minds.

Distant Dads

I can still remember my mother becoming quite sad,
every time I ask her to tell me about my dad.

She said they loved each other, but things got in the way,
I guess I was not enough to make my dad stay.

As a child I was frightened as could be,
I could not understand why my dad wasn't here with me.

Every year on my birthday when I first awake,
I know he will not see me blow out the candles on my cake.

As a teenager there was a lot I was confused about,
that's when I needed him most to help me figure things out.

Years have gone by and I graduated in the fall,
I hoped and prayed he would pick up the phone and call.

I understand he's married and has a new family,
I was the one sacrificed, how could he forget about me.

I've grown up now and a parent myself,
I will be there for my children when they need help.

When I look at other families it still makes me quite sad,
all I ever wanted in life was to know my dad.

Drugs, Tobacco and Alcohol

Reality is a tough stage to perform on everyday,
especially when barriers are always getting in the way.

People who run for cover appear to have no backbone,
can't accept the challenges of life so they disrupt their home.

Drugs or alcohol is an easy way out so it's the first road they take,
Self-denial of the facts leads them to believe there's no escape.

Tobacco the legal drug easily becomes a socially accepted crutch,
it can also be altered to give what is known as a bad rush.

It doesn't matter that all three are convicted killers who keep you low,
high first thing in the morning until your head hits the pillow.

Even though you deny the truth we all know what lies ahead,
If you don't break free the drugs or alcohol will rule until you are dead.

Taking all the new designer drugs trying to appease your peers,
Did you ever stop and think your family is on the brink of tears?

When you make the decision to get high that's really a bad call,
it hurts your love ones when you surrender to drugs, tobacco and alcohol.

I Don't Wanna Be Carjacked

I worked hard, saved my money to buy a new car, lived in a shack,
Sunroof top, chrome wheels, CD player, color is jet black.

I love to cruise the freeways, listening to good music, sunroof pulled back,
enjoying my life while I still have it, trying to keep my values in tact.

One morning the newscaster said "look what happened to Queen La Tefah,"
she was carjacked in Harlem at 3:00 a.m., they took her '95 Beamer.

Carjackers don't care if you are rich, famous and a big star,
the only thing they care about is how they're going to get your car.

What kind of person would do such a thing? He has to be wacked,
out to make fast money so he can go and buy some crack.

It's the law of the land, stay away from the hood, even in the daytime,
unemployment, poverty, poor education always breeds high crime.

Handguns, automatic weapons, always gotta watch your back,
I try hard not to fall into a trap, I won't try to fight off the attack.

If this happens to me I will just have to give up my beautiful black car,
It's not worth more than my life, sometimes they go too far.

It don't make sense for us to have to live this way, afraid of our own kids,
when something like this happens, we wonder if it was something we did.

Maybe its safer to ride a ten speed and carry around a backpack,
I just want to enjoy my car, I don't wanna be carjacked.

Let My People Go

You're trying to shatter our faith by burning our churches to the ground,
we'll keep rebuilding our churches you can't keep our spirit down.

We're standing on the promises of God this is truly our belief,
we'll ignore the attempts of your intimidation and not give into defeat.

One day our people will walk freely without having to watch their backs,
we will exercise our rights of freedom without being under attack.

We will surpass society's evils as long as we hold on to our faith,
our prayer for mankind is to let go of all their passed on hate.

Our ancestors told us of their bondage in the days of old,
we made a vow to continue their struggle by eliminating your hold.

We're educating ourselves so you flooded our neighborhoods with dope,
another form of slavery that destroys all our dreams and hope.

If we are to survive today's work force we will have to rechannel our focus,
you are making sure affirmative action will not be around to help us.

We refuse to continue being the minority people oppressed,
we only want to live our lives in harmony among all the rest.

We're becoming a tower of strength, we will prevail you know,
when will you tear down these walls of hate and let my people go.

Living In The Realm of Abuse

Love is blind is a fragment of truth, love is binding is reality.
Reality is hard to deal with sometimes so you give up your dignity.

Mind altering substance transforms love ones into a state of empty morality.
Drugs ignore your pleas for help so it can maintain complete authority.

You watch helplessly when alcohol turns significant others into strangers.
You then fall victim to their unwarranted excuses to justify their anger.

Physical abuse send you running for help in the middle of the night.
How can you ignore the last look on your children's faces was that of fright?

You live everyday with the false hope that things are going to change.
You deny the truth and continue to live day in and day out in unlimited pain.

Men dishonor themselves violating children causing them to lose self-respect.
Their minds influenced by drugs and alcohol they will soon live to regret.

Mental attacks with degrading words cause havoc on your self-esteem.
You accept excuses while intoxicated they say things they don't really mean.

Abusers always seem to take their frustrations out on their mates.
You can't right all the wrong they have done; how much more will you take?

The road to recovery is a start once they admit help is what they truly need.
All things are possible with commitment as long as they take heed.

You are not alone; a failed relationship is no reason to be ashamed.
Its time to be honest about this behavior in actuality abuse is its name.

Existing in a violent relationship trying to keep family together is of no use.
No good can ever come out of living in the realm of abuse.

My Diary

Dear Diary you are my pen pal, confidant and one of my best friends.
When it comes to revealing my most intimate moments it's you I can confide in.

I can pour my heart and soul out; I don't have to hide anything from you.
I can be open and honest all the time; every word you hold is true.

I don't have to keep feelings inside me; with you I can express myself.
I may not get all the answers I need but having you there sure does help.

You know everything that is important to me in my life.
You know when I am in love with someone or when I have a serious fight.

You know all about the things that happen to make me sad.
You know about all the terrible things I encounter that made me mad.

You also know all the people and things that made me really happy.
You know all the things I could never reveal to my mommy and daddy.

I confide in you so heavily I can't leave you lying around free.
The things you know I would never want anyone else to know about me.

When my friends and family turn to me for confidentiality.
I can express my feelings to you without ever revealing their reality.

I must keep you in a safe place for security; always under lock and key.
You are the one silent friend I can turn to, my companion forever, my diary.

March of Kings

They came forward seeking their atonement.
Ignoring responsibilities was never their intent.
And they marched.

The time came when they heard their people's cries.
Their manhood was challenged so a million black men did rise.
And they marched.

They came from all over; East, West, North and South.
Accepting the challenge they were ready for their first bout.
And they marched.

They came in large numbers their faces filled with unspoken pride.
They stood up so the world could see they had nothing to hide.
And they marched.

They came together to brainstorm and together work things out.
They will return home to teach their sons what responsibility is all about.
And they marched.

The road to change will be a long hard one.
These proud black men won't stop until the job is done.
And they marched.

Their pledge was to make our people self-sufficient.
No longer will they walk into brick walls waiting for our government.
And they marched.

Remember the day when one million black men marched on Washington.
A peaceful demonstration was step one; the first battle has just been won.
And they marched.

They wore their pride like a halo; their spirit has sprout new wings.
Brace yourself for a new generation; you've just witnessed The March of Kings.

Martin Luther King

Martin my dear departed leader if only you were still here.
I know you had a dream of united people but we still live in fear.

You were taken away from us April 4, 1968 the day of our fallen King.
This act shattered a lot of hopes about letting freedom ring.

We as a people of color are still fighting for our civil rights.
What's at the end of this tunnel of antagonism, will we ever see the light?

We're armed with education and have gone places none have gone before.
Now our government wants to stop affirmative action and close all the doors.

Everyday there is a new challenge before us in this vast discriminating nation.
Today they have a new reason to stop us, its called reverse discrimination.

At every turn we always end up being the people oppress,
we'll be fighting for equal ground forever as long as we're put to the test.

Your dream for us has not died; the hopes you gave us sets us apart.
I know you would have been proud to see the Million Man March.

My hopes soared to new heights when I first heard I had a dream,
like Moses God sent us another leader known as Dr. Martin Luther King.

Mr. President

When you were campaigning politicians said
you made promises you couldn't keep.

Some of your chosen members disappointed you,
however, you would not give in to defeat.

You stood up to your critics and held your head up proud;
not all of the "Good Old Boys" can walk so freely in a crowd.

Politicians said your wife was the one running the office;
jokingly, they called her Mrs. President.

Some people just refuse to admit you married a loving mother,
and a pretty woman who was intelligent.

No one who voted for you expected you to be perfect;
down to earth people seldom are.

If all our leaders on Capitol Hill would just work with you
I truly believe in my heart you would certainly go far.

Politicians put obstacles in your path to try to bring you down.
Being the man that you are; you braced yourself and stood your ground.

Republicans want you out of the Oval Office after serving only one term.
Take another look at your opposition; their eyes are filled with hunger.
What they don't see is in the hearts of the American people;
sometimes the short-lived live longer.

President Kennedy was the last president in my lifetime
who went all out for civil rights.
It's good to see you refuse to back down from the opposition without a fight.

Maybe the next one America put in office might make a little more sense.
No one could ever replace you, Bill Clinton, Mr. President.

New Years Day

Woke up this morning revived and feeling good.
All is peaceful in the neighborhood.

It rained all night leaving behind clean air.
I have a day off from work to relax in my lounge chair.

Family and friends call all day to wish me well.
Things are going to be different this year I can tell.

Football playoffs are intense they're putting on a good show.
Each team doing their best to make it to the super bowl.

You can smell food cooking, aroma coming from everywhere.
Neighbors preparing for family and friends to get there.

Time for a new approach to problems by finding a solution.
Making changes in my life is my New Year's resolution.

Start a new program to improve my health.
Review investments to bring me wealth.

Say good-by to the old year while holding back the tears.
Taking my new found wisdom into the new year.

No more procrastination; nothing will get in my way.
These are promises I made to myself on this New Years Day.

Plight of the Homeless

When less fortunate people approach us for help we view them as pests.
When will we take the blinders off our eyes and see these people are in distress.

Day in and day out these people with few choices aimlessly roam.
They sleep and eat where they can because they have no place to call home.

Everyday is a struggle to survive; most of them live in the fields.
Nothing to protect them from the weather and no doctors when they become ill.

We need to reach out to them a little more by raising our level of compassion.
It's time to stop thinking about others changing things and we take action.

We can't continue on our current path of all talk and not really resolving it.
We celebrate our own good fortune and ignore the fact homelessness still exist.

There are no guarantees in life you never know what your life has in store.
Our lives could take a turn for the worst and we can enter the world of the poor.

It affects all of us when these people become desperate enough to steal.
We have no idea what it is like to continuously go without a meal.

It is time for us to deal with this problem and stop turning our backs.
Reach out to someone in need and help them get their lives back on track.

This is not going to be an easy job; it may prove to be quite hard.
If you're wondering where to find wayward people just look in your backyard.

Stop waiting for the holidays to come so you will have a good reason.
This is a daily problem its not one that comes with a season.

As long as these people roam our minds will never be completely at rest.
If we all put our hearts together we can end the plight of the homeless.

Prejudice

The sad thing about prejudice is everyone has it.

The bad thing about prejudice is there's no cure for it.

The frightening thing is when a person thinks he don't have it.

What really make people nervous are the ones who show it.

The good thing about prejudice is people don't want it.

The truth about prejudice is we can all live without it.

The question is what are we going to do about it?

The challenge is how do we eradicate it?

When are the people going to get it?

The world would certainly be a better place without it.

Prejudice The Demon

I wonder if people realize how powerful you really are.
You will go to any length to destroy good people you don't care how far.

You make good people compromise their values.
You dwell in the minds of all ages; you don't care who you use.

You have roamed the earth since the beginning of time.
You make a decent place to live without your presence impossible to find.

You compromise our judicial system allowing the guilty to go free.
You also manage to cut off the branches from extended family trees.

Is there any humanly way we can every combat you.
Every time we think we've got you licked; you come back with something new.

You feed on the weak and frightened people, I don't understand why.
Your influence make children kill one another,
do you enjoy watching mothers cry?

As long as you run rampant there will never be true justice.
One day the people will all join forces against this demon called Prejudice.

Song Of The Survivors

Life thus far you've put me through the toughest tests.
You thought I would give up so you gave me no rest.

I survived every attack you sent my way.
You retreated and came more brutal another day.

A dark cloud hovered over my family covering the evils of incest.
I sank into a river of emotions that overflowed until it crest.

The ill winds of temptations infiltrated my marriage until the separation.
Our judicial system divided our union with very little deliberation.

Challenges of single parenthood were a never-ending fight.
The love of my children made me protect them to make things right.

That dark cloud hovered over my unsuspecting home again.
Why can't family see this is one of God's deadly sins.

The shadow of betrayal still follows me wherever I go.
I refuse to let it destroy me I have the strength to endure I know.

I will rise above it all; the pain has played with my self-esteem long enough.
I survived this far by trusting in God, a strong will and staying tough.

Now I see life through new eyes and I have a serene melody in my heart.
My mind and will is rejuvenated; everyday will be a brand new start.

The lyrics of life are written in the hearts of all survivors; they are my mentors.
Listen to the rhythm of our souls; this is the song of the survivors.

The Hills of San Jose

From the first moment I inhaled San Jose air,
I knew within my heart I belong there.

It was unlike no other place I had seen,
this broad metropolis yet so serene.

I was so taken in by the rainbow of faces,
people coming here from so many different places.

I believe everyone here is looking for the same thing,
a place we can call home where freedom magically rings.

It is so calming living in such a diverse society,
what other cities only dream of is San Jose's reality.

The hills surround San Jose like a mother embracing her child,
the many cultures give the city its own majestic style.

The chill of winter nights quietly lay a soft blanket of snow,
the view from my window is like a grand picture show.

Those hills standing taller than life itself in tranquil splendor,
the sight of it takes my breath away every time I step out the door.

I am here to live out the rest of my life I won't ever drift away,
I was captivated the moment I saw the hills of San Jose.

This May Be The Last Time

I feel the warmth of the summer sun.
Walk bare feet in the sand having fun.

Watch the sun set on the horizon blue.
See the sun rise after the morning dew.

Smell flowers after the wind captures their scent.
See colors of a rainbow wondering where the end went.

Climb to the top of a mountain high.
Feel the rainfall from the sky.

Hear a humming bird sing.
Watch a bald eagle spread his wings.

Sit on the porch and watch clouds go by.
Lie in the grass under a clear blue sky.

Watch the creation of honey by those little bees.
Enjoy the shade under tall oak trees.

Wake up in the morning when the rooster crows.
Go to a matinee to see a new picture show.

Pack my bags and go on an exciting trip.
Dance under the stars on a big cruise ship.

Today I am going to love life while it is still mine.
I'm not promised tomorrow this may be the last time.

When You Can't Turn Life Around

If life leaves a sour taste in your mouth then find out why,
don't contaminate others with your discontent as they pass you by.

Sometime a little change in attitude could make a difference in your life,
maybe you won't have to struggle so much, a day can go by without a fight.

Open your mind to new ideas don't get trapped in your own tunnel vision,
learn from everyone who surrounds you these are true words of wisdom.

When you see someone's approach is different doesn't mean it's all wrong,
takes what's good from both sides, unite efforts that's how you become strong.

You can create problems for yourself unnecessarily over the years,
step out of your comfort zone, accept a challenge it may save you a lot of tears.

Prepare yourself for a new generation of thoughts nothing remains the same,
every time lightening strikes dry wood it always start a new flame.

Don't intimidate others with condescending words to masquerade your needs,
remember words can be damaging when you deliberately plant bad seeds.

Life don't have to be a tug of war, dragging other people's views to the ground,
take another look at your approach to life when you can't turn life around.

Where Do I Draw The Line?

I call you every once in a while.
I always leave a message so you can return my call.

Hoping you will call before it gets to late.
I find myself feeling disappointed as I continue to wait.

When I make special plans I always include you.
You promise to show but you never come through.

The excuses you give me are getting real thin.
This relationship is not meant to happen there's no way I can win.

I know what it feels like to want something you can't have.
I never knew I could want anything or anyone this bad.

It is my denial of our relationship that makes me sad.
I have to walk away from this web of yours before I go completely mad.

Here I go wanting to pick up the phone to call you again.
When will I admit to myself you only want a friend.

If I put you in an awkward position I truly apologize.
I'm the first to admit a fool in love is not very wise.

I have to save what's left of my dignity.
I can't continue to let you make a fool out of me.

The way you are treating me is not very kind.
I ask myself over and over again where do I draw the line?

My Journey

I heard a cry for help from unknown people oppressed.
I was on the threshold of manhood; this was to be my test.
I heard the pain and suffering in their defenseless voices.
I had to answer their pathetic cries; there were no choices.

I put on my badge of honor and decided to take a proud stand.
Not knowing who was friend or foe in this divided foreign land.
I went not knowing my own government's game plan.
With no acquaintances, family or friends to hold my hand.

I never knew a country could be in such disarray.
The souls of the people were as if they had decayed.
Children carrying weapons before the age of puberty.
Will they ever know the true meaning of peace and liberty?

I saw life ascending from bodies lain on unsanitary ground.
So much death and destruction it made my head spin around.
So many babies becoming orphans daily left me astound.
The blank look on their faces said no hope could be found.

Contrary to popular beliefs there are no justified fights.
It's hard as hell to digest taking someone's precious life.
The aftermath of war is a never-ending mental battle.
It's like a cold beautiful snake with a fearless deadly rattle.

We brought all our unjust prejudices with us to this man-made hell.
We fought two wars, one with the enemy, the other among ourselves.
I didn't know which was more frightening, stepping on a hidden live wire,
or always watching my back trying to avoid a so-called friendly fire.

Will I truly ever feel complete or clean inside again?
War is a massacre of souls descending; no one ever wins.
Will we continue to destroy ourselves until the very end?
Power, greed and endless lust is how it always begins.

I returned home to what was supposed to be my land of the free.
There were no marching bands or flags waving waiting for me.
Does anyone care what this insane war has done to my head?
They only shunned me, disowned me and ridiculed me instead.

My Journey (Continued)

I thought the country that I loved would stand by my side.
No hero's homecoming for me, I only wanted to run and hide.
I was offered counseling and drugs they thought would help.
Is there a cure for this hostile rage burning inside myself?

I left here when I was called, a very proud man.
I came home altogether different; the way that I am.
Mentally devastated, shattered and always having to roam.
Cut off from my very roots; no place I can call home.

My people, my people you always hear the distant cry.
Do you ever truly hear the ones right here by your side?
Open your eyes, stop, look and take heed.
The men and women coming home from wars are in dire need.

Father you promised I would not get more than I could bear.
I know you walked every mile with me or I would still be there.
I humble myself before you Father I truly believe you care.
Restore peace to my soul inside this armor of faith that I wear.

I believe there is nothing worst than the torment I have seen.
Some things were so heart felt it knocked me to my knees.
Now I understand the written words "Thou art with me."
Viet Nam was my valley of death, the beginning of my journey.

This poem is dedicated to all the women and men who served in this devastating war. I met a lot of veterans that was affected by this war, especially after returning home. They went where their country sent them and paid a high price for their loyalty. To this day I still don't understand why we were in Viet Nam.

Andrew It's Time To Rest

Why did you decide to leave us behind?
You were always so gentle, thoughtful and kind.

You will remain in our hearts although it is stained.
One thing you couldn't take from us is the love still remained.

I know you felt like you did a dry run.
Little did you know your life had just begun?

I know you felt like you gave it your best.
Little did you know life is just an ongoing test?

I know you wanted more from life and wouldn't accept less.
I guess you made your final decision my friend.
Now Andrew its time to rest.

In Loving Memory of Andrew Wilson
Who decided to end his life before he begun to live.
1967 - 2001

Bond of the Hood

Memories can sometimes haunt us or remind us of good times
when we were young and carefree.

Memories can also replay the old love songs in our heads
reminding us of what use to be.

The funny thing about memories we can choose the good ones
and block out all the bad.

We only want to remember the ones that make us smile
not the ones that make us sad.

Going back to the hood after so many years we say to ourselves
"I can't believe I did that".

Remember the hood was our learning tree;
remember where we started and where we're at.

The hood fertilized our roots and bonded us all
for whatever reason together.

We will carry this bond all our lives
whether good, bad or indifferent forever.

Listen up; take notice we can no longer close our eyes to the truth.

We lost more comrades in drug and territory battles
than they did in Beirut.

Our love ones, acquaintances and friends me made along the way
they have never understood.

We carry the scars of battle, wisdom of experience, strength of character
and the eternal bond of the hood.

Father Remember Me

Father I come to you with a humble heart.
I lay my fears and burdens here at the altar.
I pray I honor you with the paths that I take.
Forgive me when I falter and make a mistake.

You know my heart Lord, you see through the haze.
I wonder endlessly confused in this demonic maze.
At times my mind is challenged and just runs astray.
I pray for your beacon Lord to show me the right way.

Thank you for the countless blessings over the years.
Thank you for Jesus the Son you gave so unselfishly.
His blood was shed for the sins revisited upon me.
I ask that you cleanse me with the spirit so I can see.

You have watched over my family with the greatest of care.
When things got really tough I knew you were always there.
I've run a good race through time holding on to my faith.
I knew that no matter how long it took you would wait.

I pray that my life here on earth has done some good.
My whole purpose of being Lord I hope is well understood.
Thank you for my life as it is Lord I will always praise thee.
When my time here has come to an end,
please Father remember me.

Shirley

This prayer is in a silver frame that sit on my alter that I prepared in honor of my Living God so that he may know my love.

I Had To Leave My Heart Behind

I never understood what you felt you had to prove.
When we took our vows I thought you were ready for that move.

We had our extreme highs and we had our unforgettable lows.
That's what love is surviving the heartaches and letting love grow.

If you could not give the love back the way I gave it to you.
Why did you just turn away leaving me hanging instead of being true?

I could never go back to where all the love and pain begin.
Every time I have flashbacks of the love we had I start running again.

I don't know if my heart will ever let someone else in.
Before I return to the hurt and pain I rather live in unforgivable sin.

How can love hurt so much when I thought it was meant to be?
Did you ever take a moment to see the love I had for you inside of me?

Did you even shed a tear for me or even miss the love that we had?
Or did you just go on with life as usual knowing that I was unbearably sad.

I watched all the love I had for you get carried away with the wayward wind.
I saw my heart in the eye of the storm reaching out like it was the next of kin.

I gave you everything that I have in my emotional heart to give.
You drained every fiber of my soul leaving me cold as stone trying to live.

I had to leave you baby to keep from going seriously out of my mind.
When I left you for the very last time I had to leave my heart behind.

Mama you're Finally Free

As the days go by I will feel your spirit in the wind.
When I hear the birds chirping I'll hear your melody again and again.

When I see a dove fly gracefully in the sky,
I will remember the love that was always in your eyes.

When I see the moon in the dark of night,
I will remember your loving smile shining so bright.

All the unpleasant things in your life left a little stain,
It's all over now Mama there's no more pain.

We had our good times and we also had our bad times,
But through it all Mama you made me the person that I am.

Every year when I see the flowers give brand new blooms,
I will remember your love and in God's time I will see you soon.

I wanted to spend more time with you doing all that we can,
I had to cancel all those engagements because God had other plans.

You traveled a long road Mama and kept your heart in tack,
God called you home saying welcomes my child and doesn't look back.

I see the clouds passing by spraying rain to clean the tainted air,
It leaves a beautiful rainbow behind to remind me that God is always there.

Now safely home in your new garden of love Mama always remember me,
I'll hold your resurrection in my heart always, Mama you're finally free.

My Little White House

My neighbors are like a beautiful garden.
A wide variety of flowers all in full bloom.

A little paradise where a lot of God's little creatures gather.
As if this were their own private living room where nothing matters.

A place where many different languages are spoken and heard.
We all know we'll apart of a unique family bond without speaking a word.

Everyone's home is all neat and clean with a rainbow of colors.
Here we all swim in a sea of pride without a bore.

The hummingbirds showing up every twenty minutes for nourishment.
In their array of colors flying gracefully as a God sent.

There is always something to do around here that keeps me running about.
Nothing is more relaxing than sitting on the front porch of my little white house.

No Longer Under Attack

Father I have lived in enemy territory all my days.
I have tried to follow the rules of engagement in every way.
I had to take up arms against my demons forcing them to retreat.
Even when I lost a battle I knew how to lay my burdens down.
I waived the blood stained banner of Jesus as I stood my ground.

There were many times I became a prisoner of war.
Never once did I deny my God and willingly surrender.
All I gave up to my demons was my name, rank and number.
I survived on the promises of God forever stored in my heart.
God said believe in me, trust only in him, his love for me will never part.
I was cleansed in the Holy Spirit; I knew then that God loved me most.
One day I will stand at the gates of heaven as his divine host.

I have run my last mile praising Jesus' name every step of the way.
I have labored in the sufferings of mankind until my judgement day.
If I have earned favor in the eyes of God he will show me the way.
I will go rejoicing praising his name now that I am home to stay.

Raise me up Lord as I lay down my weapons stained with life.
I did the best I knew how when I became a woman, a mother and a wife.
I knew through it all that no matter what happened Lord you had my back.
I am ready to climb the stairway to heaven now I am no longer under attack.

Broken Heart Blues

Old wise people constantly say only the strong will survive.
I must be a strong woman because I survived all your lies.
I gave you all the love I had in my heart, this you can't deny.
I sit back and wonder what went wrong why did the love die?

When we met you were down on your luck trying your best to deal.
I opened up my heart to you, sharing everything I had that was for real.
You turned my pockets inside out then ran and jumped behind the wheel.
Leaving me lost, shamed and bewildered did you really have to steal?

I am not going to hang my head in shame, you'll pass my way again.
I only wish you the best baby no matter whatever shape you're in.
I thought we had a good thing, never thought I would be the one to lose.
Here I go again fighting all these crazy emotions with these broken heart blues.

You will never find another good woman who will love and honor thee.
I was the best thing that you had going when you realized that I would be free.
I took a shell of a man and made you a comfortable home and fine as can be.
What are you going to do when you can no longer use me?

I gave you money when you needed it, bought you a new car too.
Dressed you up in fine clothes, jewelry and even bought matching shoes.
This is a sad story told over and over again, I thought I could never be used.
You caught me by surprised baby, leaving me with these broken heart blues.

Today I Cried

I woke up this morning realizing today I have a brand new start.
I am going to pray until I have a healthy mind, body and heart.

I don't know why I started to cry, no one had recently left me or died.
My emotions was running all over the place.
Was I crying for myself or for the whole human race.

I had so many feelings suppressed inside of me that I didn't want to address.
I could not run from these feelings until they leave me there will be no rest.

I silently talk to God all the time thanking him for my blessings
and asking for strength.
My mind plays all kinds of dirty tricks on me telling me its no use to repent.

I cried for my family to soften their struggle with obstacles here and there.
I cried for my children knowing the road they must travel
and the pain they share.

I cried hoping they never forget that I will always care.
I cried for the sick and homeless and ask God to end their despair.

I cried for peace to come into the homes of people everywhere.
I cried for all living things flying in the air, running on land
or swimming in the sea.

I cried for the beauty in the world like the mountains, the rainbows
and the weeping willow tree.

The tears kept running down my face as though they were
trying to set themselves free.

I realized I was crying for my savior not to pass me by,
to always remember you and me.

The Beauty of You

Being a father has it challenges but love will see you through.
It can make your heart sing with joy and again can make you blue.

Sometimes parenthood is unexpected and sometimes we choose.
Sometimes we overcome the difficulties and sometimes we lose.

When I held you in my arms for the first time I knew it was a love everlasting.
It was a love that came naturally and was also mine for the asking.

I was so proud of all your accomplishments and overcoming peer temptations.
Now I watch you with your sons and daughters your precious little creations.

You are a wonderful father and you are in your children lives to stay.
The bond is so strong with the love of them nothing can ever drive it away.

This day was set aside to honor you in every possible way.
Today stand proud in your achievements son and have a happy father's day.

Having you, keeping you safe, and being worthy of your love was my greatest feat.
I am truly blessed to have you as a son, when you came along my life was complete.

Every seed you sow my son is an extension of the love that you always knew.
You kept it together against all the odds Son, that's the beauty of you.

Loving You More Everyday,

Mom.

Happy Father's Day Son wish I was there to share it with you.

This poem was written especially for my three handsome sons, Harold, Avery and DarVale. They are great fathers doing the best they can. They love their children. I guess I must have done something right.

We Could Have Made it Work

Why didn't you tell me how much you really hurt?
It was never my intentions to treat you like dirt.

If I caused you a lot of pain it was not meant to be,
I took it for granted that it would always be you and me.

Why did you have to hold everything painful inside?
If you would have just talk to me you would still be by my side.

I never saw our love falling through the crack,
I know if we really work at it we can find our way back.

I know now that I made a lot of stupid mistakes,
I will wait for you always no matter how long it takes.

Maybe I deserve the pain I am feeling for all my neglect,
I still have the love in my heart that started the first day we met.

I let a lot of not so important things now go straight to my head,
I will give it all away without a second thought if I could have you instead.

How can you just walk away without giving our love another try?
I came home to find you gone without telling me good-by.

I could never apologize enough baby for being such a selfish jerk,
If only you would have believed in our love we could have made it work.

When I See God

When I open my eyes in the morning and feel the warmth of the sun rays
shinning through my window.

When I go for my morning walks breathing clean air while listening
to birds singing in the trees.

When I see a mother walking holding her child witnessing
the love vibrantly shining in her eyes.

When I look at the mountains surrounding me in a miracle
color of green standing mighty while housing little creations.

When I pick the fruit from my trees that nourishes my body
with the taste of sweetness soothing my soul.

When I step into a warm bath to cleanse myself from the spoils of my
daily encounters embracing the healing spirit.

When I hear the voice of love ones sharing their lives with me,
praying with me and just plain loving me.

When I feel the wind blowing all around me in a prelude to the rains
that cleans the air and quenches my thirst.

When I find the strength to endure the pain and suffering life
sometimes bring and emerge a victor in my own rights.

When all the wars come to an end and all the armies return home to once
again to live in peace and wash off the stench it leaves behind.

When the bells of freedom ring loud enough for the whole world to hear.
When families are safe in their homes no longer living in fear.

When the spirit anoints me with unending blessings I am unable to count.
When I am lifted up carried in the spirit as my reward for believing.

This is when I see God.

When You Look at Me Daddy

Did I lure you to my bed with my excitement whenever you came home?
Did the hugs and kisses of a little girl spark an arousal when we were alone?

Did you not know that your seed would grow into a beautiful flower?
You are suppose to nurture and cultivate the flower when it blooms not bother.

The admiration in your eyes always showed the love I truly needed so much.
Although you have loving feelings there are parts you're never suppose to touch.

In your twisted mind you want my feelings for you to be that of pure lust.
If you look deep enough you'll see that you destroyed all my sense of trust.

Now I carry around with me a painful scar, one that was cut so deep.
I have no sweet memories, the thought of you daddy only make me weep.

I'm not to be dragged around and used like your personal little love caddy.
Remember it's my life you're destroying when you look at me Daddy.

When You're A Child

As a baby my Mom and Dad held me in their arms.
They love me and protected me from all harms.

Speaking my first words was a great big thrill.
Eating my first ice cream cone gave me a chill.

Riding my first bike was a lot of fun.
I like playing ball with Dad and watching him run.

I was really scared on my first day of school.
I made new friends and learned new rules.

Life is like walking down a long scary mile.
Life has a lot of surprises when you're a child.

Reflections

Today I went to a studio to have some pictures taken.
When I looked into my mature face a lot of old feelings were awaken.

The timelines in my face took me back down memory lane.
Had I truly lived my life to its fullest or a lot of it in vane.

I looked into my eyes where I saw all the challenges of time.
The stretch marks of motherhood that delivered beautiful children, all mine.

I saw the many faces of insecurities, old relationships, love and pain.
I remembered the road to hell and the detour that brought me back again.

I also saw a new beginning with hopes and dreams of no rejections.
I saw all these things in the portrait of myself and in my reflections.

I Wonder

Lord, today as I spent time in my little nurtured garden
filled with beautiful colors.
How can someone look at all the beauty that surrounds them
and not feel your presence?

I wonder

Feeling the cool of morning so quiet and serene
with the dew of the night leaving its reminder.
How can someone not know your spirit passed over
his or her home during the night?

I wonder.

When I hear the birds singing in the trees
and see butterflies spreading their colorful wings.
Little creatures going about their daily chores of life's contribution.
How can we not see you?

I wonder.

When I feel my heart beating with life
and the blood running through my veins so rapidly.
Family surrendering unconditional love; witness your power.
How can I not love you?

I wonder.

With all the greatness that you've shown us unselfishly;
your sacrifice Lord from way up yonder.
Why are there so much killing, hatred, disbelief, jealousy, violations,
and broken homes?

I wonder.

It All Starts With You

Shout my people, stand up and be heard.
Don't turn and run like a wounded bird.

Spread your wings like the graceful wild hawk.
Don't be the prey, rise up, strut your stuff and proudly walk.

Look forward, make a difference, bring about a new change.
Remember our history when our ancestors were bonded in chains.

Embrace life, respect lives, show the true natural beauty that lies within.
Lift up your powerful voices; this universe won't deny the black skin.

There is only one way out of an intrusive dark living hell.
Redirect your priorities. Don't raise your children from a jail cell.

Don't build stumbling blocks; build endless roads my kin.
Harness the love of life, righteous people will pass your way again.

Exercise everyday undying faith and power of righteousness instead.
Get intoxicated with the Holy Spirit and make Jesus your daily bread.

Let your talents explode immensely, build empires with your abilities.
Reward your victories, no matter how small. This is your social security.

I had a vision of a garden where families were again made whole.
The streets were sparkling clean, children playing, and no more ghettos.

I know that this vision is on its way to becoming quite true.
It all begins right here, right now my sisters and brothers.
It all starts with you.

Rodd

Your going down on 10/4 left all our hearts in rut.
With each passing moment we remain all choked up.

Our prayers are truly surrounding you with great faith.
Our anticipation keeps rising as we continue to wait.

God answered all our prayers reminding us he's never in a rush.
We ask God to grant our prayers by keeping you here with us.

You are here with us today by grace you can surely bet.
Although he loves you truly God is not ready for you yet.

Right now the nights are silent and days can be quite long.
Keep your chin up partner rest assure that you are not alone.

There was never a doubt I'm sure you always knew.
That in your time of despair we will all be here for you.

Rodd every time you see the flashing lights of the red, white and blue.
Remember the love is real partner that we are sending out to you.

Your AMR Brothers and Sisters
(American Medical Response)

This poem was written for Rodd Van de Wark. A dedicated EMT who was hit by a car while riding his motorcycle. Rodd survived but will never walk again.

I am Woman

God took a rib from man and said a woman you will be.
You will love and care for man as you stand before me.

You will bear sacred fruit from the seed of the man.
Make a home for your family and let love rule the land.

He made me the glue that would hold the family together.
I am the cool of day and the warmth of night in any kind of weather.

I will take the harvest from the land to give my family a feast.
I am the backbone of my family's courage that will never retreat.

I will honor my home by keeping it safe, loving and clean.
I am the foundation of man, on God's word I will lean.

I will make courageous women out of beautiful little girls.
I will raise leaders, teachers, and rulers of this world.

My job is endless, very little time for me to rest.
Each day comes with challenges putting my faith to the test.

I truly know now why God gave woman life.
It was the added strength man needed from a wife.

He knew if anyone could beat the temptations of life I can.
I am the hopes and the dreams of man, I am woman.

Words of Wisdom

Time to Get Things Done

Well I guess I'll try to find the time.
So what you got to do is get things done.

While you're alive and well.
Cause once you're sick and can't move to do the undone.
How can you get it done?

The creator gave us the will power to do what we want to do.
So let us do it cause once we're gone.
We won't be there to do the undone.

Time fly and our life is like a breath of air.
After we're gone how can we get it done?

So make time to get it done.
Cause your neighbor won't do it for you.
Your mailman won't do it for you.

Just make up your mind and use your will power
and do it, get it done.

Angelina Martinez

I am the daughter of Andress Orona and Maria Orona. I understand they were both Spanish American. I have six brothers and four sisters. We are a very happy family I should say. Being that I was the fifth child I was always busy. Always working. When I wasn't working I would sit and work with my hands. Sewing, embroidering, and housecleaning. I was always reading writing or drawing. Now that I am older I love reading. I am married with three boys and three girls. I write when I am resting and relaxing. I am seventy-four years old, born and raised in Colorado. I now live in San Jose, California. I love it in San Jose because of my breathing, nice weather and very agreeable to me.

ISBN 1-41204207-0

Made in the USA
Las Vegas, NV
07 August 2021